Social Media in Action

Social Media in Action

Comprehensive Guide for Architecture, Engineering, Planning and Environmental Consulting Firms

Written by Amanda Walter and Holly Berkley

Illustrated by Charly Nelson

 Watermelon Books

Watermelon Books
1520 Dale Street
San Diego, CA 92102-1519

ISBN 9780985146917

Library of Congress Control Number: 2012932774

Keywords: Social media, A/E, online marketing, thought leadership, online community, social network, blogging, search engine optimization

Table of Contents

Foreword to Social Media in Action

"Wow" is all I can say when it comes to the content of Amanda Walter's and Holly Berkley's new book, "Social Media in Action: Comprehensive Guide for Architecture, Engineering, Planning and Environmental Consulting Firms." This book is chock full of helpful information and explanations of all of the social media options available to design firms today.

There's a lot of help here for those who want to understand all of this stuff and how it ties together marketing-, PR, and brand building-wise for any firm in our business. The specificity of instruction will give anyone—novice or master alike—a clear direction in how to use these communication tools that are revolutionizing our professions and industry today.

One of the great things about this book is that it is so much more than just the informed opinions of the authors. It is based on significant primary and secondary research. The authors' conclusions and advice is well-grounded—sure to help convince the most skeptical architect, engineer, or scientist of the rationale for what they need to do.

Read on to learn all about Social Media in Action!

Mark C. Zweig
Founder & CEO
ZweigWhite, LLC
Fayetteville, Arkansas

Acknowledgements

The idea for an A/E industry-specific book on social media was first dreamed up by ZweigWhite. I may not have ever considered writing this book if it weren't for the suggestion by Chris Parsons. As an ambitious entrepreneur and advocate for A/E industry leaders to embrace social media, it is no wonder that ZweigWhite originally approached him. Chris has a vision for our industry and, lucky for us, a passion and skill for leading us all to that horizon. I am so thankful to Chris for referring ZweigWhite to me and for the other doors that he's opened on my behalf. I look forward to reading his book one day —whenever he chooses to write it.

As I considered how I would approach a book on social media, I knew I would need more technical and analytical depth — immediately I thought of my close friend Holly Berkley. Holly not only brought this knowledge set, but her experience in having already written two books made the process a more comfortable one. For some, the idea of working with a good friend may be a concern, but there was never a second thought and collaborating with Holly has been the most fun of this project.

Holly and I developed a great relationship with the editors at ZweigWhite. Alan Ostner, our editor, challenged us with a tight timeline and managed to keep us on track. We know that Alan and his team's involvement have resulted in a stronger book. It was a disappointment to us all that we weren't able to publish the book through ZweigWhite, but we remain grateful for the opportunity they created. So, thank you ZweigWhite, specifically Alan Ostner, Kira Hiltz, Grace Pennington, Christina Zweig, Eric Howerton and Mark Zweig.

We also need to recognize Charly Nelson who created the fun illustrations that add a visual layer to our text. She was also an occasional researcher, brainstormer and tie-er of loose ends. We may not have made our final deadline without her talent and support. A thank you to Erinn and David Burch for being an early sounding board and to the many people who thoughtfully answered our questions and queries, and responded to our discussion threads and surveys. Many of these are recognized in the pages to come, but we appreciate everyone who contributed their story to this project.

It's most important that we acknowledge the people who were affected by this project each day. Our families put up with and accommodated our very early mornings, late evenings, working on the weekends and during vacations. To our husbands and kids Brian, Riley and Rory Walter and Keith, Calvin and Charlie Berkley, thank you for your flexibility and patience with us. We love you so much.

-Amanda Walter

Common Web-based Resources

Social Networks:
Facebook.com
LinkedIn.com
Twitter.com
Meetup.com
Foursquare.com
Quora.com
Pinterest.com
SlideShare.com
YouTube.com
Flickr.com

Bookmarking Platforms:
Digg.com
StumbleUpon.com
Reddit.com
Del.icio.us

Blog platforms:
Blogger.com
Bloglines.com
Tumblr.com
Wordpress.com
Drupal.org
MoveableType.org

Community platforms:
Ning.com
SocialGo.com
CrowdVine.com
Spuz.com

Social Media Management tools:
Tweetdeck
Hootsuite
SproutSocial.com
Ping.fm
SocialOomph.com

Link Shorteners:
Bit.ly
Tiny.url
Goo.gl

Social Media Monitoring tools:
Google.com/alerts
Google Keywords (link changes frequently)
Google.com/analytics
Radian6.com
SocialMention.com
Sysomos.com
BeeVolve.com

Stock imagery and photography:

Veer.com

SXC.hu

Gettyimages.com

Dreamstime.com

Survey tools:

Surveymonkey.com

PollDaddy.com

Instantsurvey.com

Zoomerang.com

Social Media News Release Tools:

PRweb.com

PitchEngine.com

Pressitt.com

Presskitn.com

AEC Social Media Tips:

Facebook.com/AECIdeaExchange

How A/E Firms Use Social Media

respondants

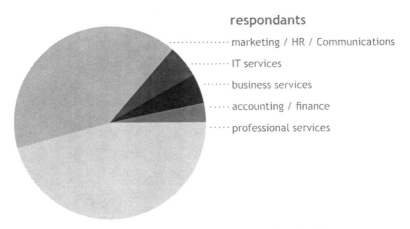

.... marketing / HR / Communications
.... IT services
.... business services
...... accounting / finance
...... professional services

firm size

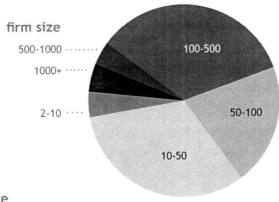

500-1000 ....
1000+ ......
2-10 ....

100-500
50-100
10-50

internet presence

100% have a website
73% on LinkedIn
48% use email marketing
45% on Facebook
36% on Twitter
20% are active on industry sites
16% have a blog
0.5% have a youtube channel

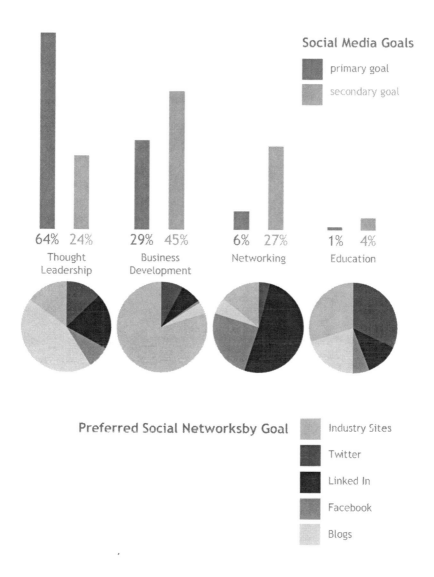

Social Media Goals

■ primary goal

■ secondary goal

| 64% | 24% | 29% | 45% | 6% | 27% | 1% | 4% |
| Thought Leadership | | Business Development | | Networking | | Education | |

Preferred Social Networks by Goal

■ Industry Sites

■ Twitter

■ Linked In

■ Facebook

■ Blogs

Results from the Social Media in Action
survey conducted by ZweigWhite.

Chapter 1
Focus on the End Result

"I don't have time."
"We don't need it."
"We just haven't gotten around to it yet."
"I don't know where to start."

We interviewed hundreds of architecture, engineering and planning firms of all sizes across the U.S. during January and February 2011 about their use of social media. There were many similar responses. The firms claimed a lack of time, resources and understanding of social media tools, as well as intimidation by the vastness of the social media space as primary factors for not yet integrating a social media strategy into their communications efforts.

While many A/E firms are watching from the sidelines, cautiously dipping their toes into the waters of social media, there are also a handful of A/E professionals who've already dived into social media and are riding that wave with some exciting results. These social media savvy professionals are watching their efforts exponentially ripple throughout the industry in powerful ways. They are successfully branding themselves as thought leaders in the industry by turning their social media connections into their most powerful advocates.

But like any tactic, the results are always better when they are directly connected to business objectives. And while new A/E professionals are finding their way into social media each day, these vehicles are not reaching everyone, yet. As a result, social technologies are an effective complement to the traditional (and largely off-line) tactics that firms have relied on for generations.

One of the major driving factors leading firms to investigate the effectiveness of social media as a communications or marketing platform (especially for smaller and/or new firms) has been the recession. "At the beginning of 2009, our phone stopped ringing," shares Laura Davis, AIA principal and director of marketing for HPD Architects in Dallas, Texas.[1] "It became apparent when 197 people showed up for a pre-submittal meeting that our chance for success in winning the project was dwindling. We realized we had to take action to bring in business." HPD included social media as a way to support their face-to-face networking and to expand the reach and influence of the firm's brand.

---

1   http://www.hpdarch.com/

Howard Blackson, principal and director of planning for San Diego, California-based PlaceMakers[2], a multidisciplinary planning and urban design firm with seven principals located in seven different cities, also points to social media as an asset for today's economic climate. He refers to social media as not only a way to conduct research and distribute thoughts and ideas, but as the core of their "New Economy" business model, which relies on the internet and social technologies to function with no overhead, no full-time office staff or central office. For PlaceMakers, social media tools allow them to run a more efficient business, bringing in expertise from all over the U.S. and Canada to easily collaborate on a single project.

Social media tools enhance the efficiency of both internal and external communication needs in the A/E industry. A single tweet or post is not only quicker than traditional forms of communication, but can reach more people faster and has a longer "shelf-life."

According to a 2011 survey from the University of Massachusetts Dartmouth Center for Market Research[3], more companies than ever view social media as an essential asset to business communications, with 86% reporting that social media technologies were "very important" to their business and marketing strategies in 2010. According to the survey, 71% of businesses used Facebook in 2010, 59% used Twitter and more than half surveyed blogged. Of this group, 85% view Facebook as successful in helping them meet their business goals, while a whopping 93% report message boards as a successful tactic.

---

2 http://placemakers.com
3 http://www.umassd.edu/cmr/studiesandresearch/socialmediaadoptionsoars

As one A/E social media advocate, Vik Duggal (@VikDug), says "The internet is about 17 years old, just about to graduate high school and is about to really blow up." Social media is even younger. The fact is, we don't know exactly how this technology will be useful to move businesses forward — the landscape is changing too rapidly to predict. However, we can say with some certainty that this medium is not going away. Social media has become an essential piece of most industry's overall communications strategy — and it is quickly infiltrating the world of design and planning as well. Professionals are sharing ideas on Twitter, leveraging connections on LinkedIn, promoting their expertise on blogs — and seeing measurable return on investment for their efforts.

Today's social media tools aren't only about technology. They are a direct response of today's business world where communications happen in real time. Think of social media as the new cell phone. Just as each and every one of your employees and consultants has a direct cell phone number to power their everyday business and communications, social media can also be leveraged for this purpose — but with a longer and stronger lifespan than a single phone call. But unlike a phone call that is between a closed or private group, social media communications allow for outside input and influence, which will help your ideas and your business expand and thrive. Social media offers the ultimate "listening tool" to gain honest input from stakeholders, feedback on your projects and your firm, as well as discover and identify industry thought leaders.

When social media tools are leveraged in the right community setting, whether that includes employees of an organization, a group of people with a common interest or goal or a community of residents sharing the same town or neighborhood, members are compelled to interact and share their perspectives. Listening to those conversations and ensuring that you are engaging on topics that matter most to your core audience is the essential ingredient for making full use of social media as a multi-directional communications tool.

This new way of thinking is an opportunity for all businesses to reorganize their overall communication strategy, decision-making authority and how information flows out to the public, clients, sub-consultants and employees. During your deep dive into social media, you will interact with customers and colleagues in a way you have never done before, and as a result you will start to build deeper relationships. Ideally, these deeper connections will be the online advocates who will carry your message further than you ever could have imagined on your own. After all, people do business with people, not impersonal mission statements, statics, websites and corporate logos. This new form of media is not a trend. It is the way businesses communicate.

Where do I start?

Time and intimidation were the main reasons businesses gave us for not having integrated social media into their communication strategies. Firms said they were so busy running their business and day to day operations that taking extra time to update a blog, find connections on LinkedIn or post a tweet was just too much. Since the industry is on the tail end of a major recession, most firms' priorities are on finding new work by being actively engaged in traditional offline connections and networking events.

Social media isn't a stand-alone program, it should come alongside a firm's strategies and business objectives that are already in place. Once you know what you are trying to accomplish, the most important piece of advice for jumping into the social media world is this: You don't have to be everywhere. It's better to have a strong, influential voice on a handful of social networks where your target audience lives than to try to keep up a presence on all of them. There are so many channels of information available; not only would trying to excel at each be overwhelming but it is impossible. Trying to be everything to everyone will not help you be effective in your social media use. In fact, it will achieve the opposite. It will dilute your overall influence in your online social circles. Focus your approach on a specific objective.

Successful use of social media for the A/E industry is not about the quantity of friends, followers, fans, posts and tweets, but rather about the quality of relationships you build and nurture online.

scattered   focused

Getting company "buy-in"

Before you sign up for your first Twitter account or register a name for your blog, define what your firm's overall communication goals are. Just like any marketing and communication vehicle, you have to plan for how you will use social media and how you will measure the success of your efforts.

You should also recognize that there is a misconception about social media, that engagement is cheap or even free. Although the social media tools themselves are free, building solid online community profiles takes company buy-in, organization and an investment in time and resources. Your firm's social media can not be run by your high-school aged child or some random intern. What goes out on the social networks must reflect your company's intellect, capability, brand, mission and be aligned with your overall business goals. Therefore the content and messaging needs to be managed by someone with a vested interest and love of the company and the topic at hand. Social media, when used correctly, can effectively support the communications for most groups within your organization, from PR and marketing to research and development and knowledge management to internal communications and recruiting.

The first step

Start with the end in mind. It's essential to understand your goals and objectives. These will drive the decisions around your target audience and what you are trying to get them to do.

If you do not know your goals, conduct a thorough analysis to set them. There are several widely published methodologies for goal setting, like the Strengths, Weaknesses, Opportunities and Threats (SWOT) analysis that can help you narrow your focus; or the SMART method — Specific, Measurable, Attainable, Realistic and Time sensitive — which is an acronym to help you check that your goals are result-oriented. Regardless of how you approach it, this step is essential. Before starting any communications engagement with our clients — whether we are looking into social media or any other marketing or communications initiative — we begin with a question and answer session to get to the heart of what they want to achieve, so that we can determine what strategies and vehicles are best suited for their goals. See the Objective and Strategy Setting sidebar for an outline of questions that drive these conversations and tips for setting objectives.

There is an old advertising adage that states a person needs to see a message seven to 12 times before they commit it to memory. It is important to find multiple ways of reaching your audience to make your messages stick. Social media should not be an isolated program and it should not replace your existing communications channels, rather it should integrate with them. Your social networks are simply communications channels. The content that you use on the social web should pull from, complement and promote the pieces of your existing marketing programs, such as your newsletters, direct mail and events.

Finally, before starting a social media campaign you must be prepared for flexibility. Social media tools and rules change frequently. Although you are not expected to be a social media expert, your company must be able to make a quick decision and respond in real time to crises as well as positive PR opportunities that arise.

Proper use of social media is about decentralized decision-making where everyone in your company can contribute and have a voice. However, before letting just anyone in your organization tweet or post on your company's behalf, defining guidelines and core messaging is essential. Setting up the right internal structure and goals before you engage in the social space is key to making it work for your company. We'll get into internal behind-the-scenes tactics for generating ideas, recruiting contributors and empowering employees in Chapter 4.

As a professional service firm, you rely on the knowledge and success of individuals within the company as a pillar of the firm's reputation. In Chapter 5, you'll find strategies that are being used at some of the most recognizable firms that are positioning their experts in front of their brand. We'll address the risks and benefits of this approach, how some are embracing their thought leaders and the changes they are seeing because of it.

Social media tools continue to grow and evolve based on the needs of today's business user. The most exciting thing about social media is that unlike any other form of media, you can track the results of your effort instantly. As you engage in social media, you'll learn that a simple adjustment in the way you compose a blog post headline, or the time of day you tweet can make a significant impact on the results you will see.

Objective and Strategy Setting Worksheet

Jumping into social media without forethought and planning is perhaps the biggest, and most common, mistake that A/E firms make. Without an objective and a strategy, there is no real way to measure, test, achieve success or determine failure. We use the principles of Strengths, Weaknesses, Opportunities and Threats (SWOT) combined with the information we've come to rely on for marketing or communications campaigns to help assess the landscape and zoom in on a good approach. This fact-finding assessment can take a general, firmwide focus or it can be specific to each market sector or service offering.

Establish Objectives

What is your mission statement, values and/or brand attributes?

What are your business goals? What are your marketing goals? What is the reputation that you aspire to have?

What parts of your business support these goals? Examples are core competencies and differentiators.

Who in your firm is instrumental to reaching these goals in roles such as a subject matter expert or inspiring leader?

What has the firm done and/or is currently doing to advance toward these goals?

Who are your clients? Who is the decision maker of these client firms and who are the influencers? What is this influencing-person's background? What does their job entail?

Who are your competitors? How are they communicating? Is it effective?

Are there sensitive issues or topics that perhaps we need to keep in mind or avoid talking about in public?

Establish a Strategy

What does success look like?

What assets are unique to your firm? These might be research and development, image library, events, marketing programs, breakthrough projects.

What are your resources that can be assigned to this effort? Examples are in-house staff and outsourced resources like agencies or consultants.

Who are these resources and what is their background, areas of expertise, interests? How much time are they allowed to spend on it?

What networks or organizations are your firm and/or its leaders actively involved in? What is the nature of the involvement such as a sponsor or board member?

As you engage in the tactics outlined in this book, we'd like to hear how you are doing. Share your ideas or ask questions at the AEC Idea Exchange Page on Facebook (http://www.facebook.com/ AECIdeaExchange).

Chapter 2
Finding Your Target Audience

By the time you finish reading this sentence, there will be 700 new posts on Facebook. By the time you finish reading this chapter, there will be 1 million new tweets. With more than 1.9 billion Internet users world wide[1], watching millions of videos, creating millions of blogs and updating posts, status updates, and comments on a daily basis, finding your target audience in the sea of social media can feel overwhelming.

Stop. Take a deep breath. Realize that in order to be successful on the social web, you do not have to be everything to everyone. Or everywhere for that matter. In fact, no one can conquer every online social network. There is simply too much information flowing every second. So rather than trying to tackle every social network at once, focus on the handful of social spaces where your target audience is most active.

As you start using social media to find and communicate with different audiences, you will quickly discover that some social networks provide more immediate benefits to your overall goals than others do. You may also discover that it can take a combination of social networks to promote your message most efficiently. Because online communications are more measurable and trackable than traditional forms of communication, the more you listen and engage on different social networks, the more you will be able to refine your efforts to maximize efficiency and attain your desired goals. (You'll learn how to track, measure and evaluate your social media efforts more in Chapter 7.)

PlaceMakers, who we introduced in Chapter 1, is a multidisciplinary firm primarily focused on the reformation of municipal zoning codes, as well as master planning and urban design for private developers. Through social media use and engagement, they have discovered that it takes a combination of social tools and messaging to reach their audiences and goals.

Scott Doyon, Atlanta, Georgia-based principal and director of marketing of PlaceMakers, LLC describes effective social media outreach as a delicate balance of several tools. He advises that A/E professionals look at their social media profiles and fan bases as a tool box. The more you engage on the sites and understand how they work and help the lives of your audiences, the better you will understand which tool to use, and when.

On any social networking site, such as Twitter and LinkedIn you can easily search by keyword*, topic, job function or company name and you'll be presented with a list of tweets, profiles, pages, groups and so on. Once you identify where your target audience is, take some time to listen.

This is a strategy that Christine Morris, communications and special projects coordinator of Construction Specialties, Inc.[2], a Muncy, Pennsylvania-based manufacturer of specialty architectural building products for interiors of hospitals, schools, office buildings, airports and stores has found success doing. "Our target audience is made up of customers, potential customers and other influencers," explains Morris. "Our first step in deciding which networks to use was to spend some time watching, listening and researching to see where this target audience was spending their time and where they were posting[*] on a consistent basis. We simply met them where they are."

Think of joining a new social networking group as stepping into a cocktail party where you don't know anyone. You wouldn't start loudly announcing your business and latest projects the second you stepped foot in the door. Not only would this be rude, but it would be a complete turn off to all the other guests. Instead, take smaller steps. Listen. Ask questions. Find out who the key influencers are in that group and get in their good graces. Also, pay attention to how the group talks, the lingo they use and how they interact with each other. You want to fit in.

Never directly push your business. Instead, contribute meaningful information that your target audience is seeking. Don't be afraid to give it away for free. Encourage dialogue that helps position you as a knowledgeable person in your industry and as someone who cares about others' thoughts, problems, concerns and opinions. Spend

---

2   http://www.c-sgroup.com

Be subtle

Listen

Ask questions

See who is most influential

Be patient

Be relevant

Be sincere

Have fun

Social Media Tips from Cocktail Party Etiquette

more of your time on social sites talking to people, building relationships, sharing resources that aren't your own products or services than you spend promoting yourself and your company. Through this type of engagement and understanding of the audiences, you will be more likely to capture the right kind of attention, along with trust and loyalty.

Once you are an accepted member of the group, test out new approaches and dialogues. Have fun with it. After all, social networking is still in its infancy as a field of interest and study. Best practices and tactics in the field are continuing to evolve. This is especially true in the A/E industry, where many industry folks are still tip-toeing in.[3]

Focus on relevant, quality messaging, not quantity, to attract your audience

In specialized fields like the design and construction industries, quality trumps quantity every time. In other words, it's better to have a few hundred Twitter followers* who are your core audience and care about what you have to say, than to have thousands of followers that will never notice you or become your online advocates by retweeting what you have to say. The same idea holds true with blogging*. Its best to have well-crafted, thought out blog posts that convey your brand messaging while providing insightful opinions and information than to post mindless chatter every day. It's the quality posts that will get forwarded, linked to, picked up by various RSS feeds* and help your online presence grow.

Understanding not only who your target audience is, but why they are engaged on a specific social network, is important. You want to understand what kind of information they are seeking in a particular social space and be able to provide that to them. For example, your Facebook friends* may want to see different types of information than those who subscribe to your blog. Though testing and tracking

3 http://www.cubitplanning.com/blog/2010/06/5-reasons-why-aec-industry-is-2-years-behind-adopting-social-media/

Building a focused social presence and crafting quality content will generate a targeted following that is more likely to engage and help share your messages.

which types of posts and information gain the most feedback in the form of comments, likes* or shares*, you will be able to optimize each social communication channel to benefit each audience, and therefore get closer to reaching your specific business goals.

A 2011 study by Razorfish[4] found that among all social networks, friends, followers and fans cited "feeling valued" as the most important element of engaging with a company online. Therefore it isn't just about providing your audience with the type of information they seek; "companies should worry less about building out numerous channels and touch points and more about ensuring each customer interaction communicates value," Razorfish says.

Ensuring value and quality posts is something PlaceMakers, LLC seems to weave effortlessly into their communications. The principals of PlaceMakers create well-thought-out blog posts that generate emotion and response, while they also fit powerful observations into 140 characters or less on Twitter. Creating a message that stirs people to respond is what social media is all about. After all, social media is

---

4   http://liminal.razorfish.com/

designed to spark dialogue between individuals to create a feeling of community. It is not a tool for simply pushing company announcements and press releases. Those types of posts and tweets are less likely to succeed in the social media space.

"We see ourselves less as individual planners, designers, marketers, etc. and more as cultivators of community," says PlaceMaker's Doyon. "Instead of just writing for other planners, we're building relationships with environmentalists, developers, city boosters, bike and pedestrian advocates and all kinds of other folks who care about community improvement."

PlaceMakers has cast a pretty wide net to cover their target audiences. But they don't do this by having one marketer or sales person doing all the tweeting, posting and chatting. Instead, PlaceMakers is able to reach many different types of audiences with valuable, thoughtful information, because they allow each team member to blog, tweet and post about subjects that are most important to them. This approach helps pave the way for each team member to begin establishing themselves as potential thought leaders in their specific areas of interest and expertise.

Deborah Reale, community manager and marketing specialist at Reed Construction Data (RCD) of Norcross, Georgia[5], has developed a similar social media strategy for Twitter. Rather than trying to push messages out and listen to all the feedback and chatter at once, she recommends segmenting Twitter followers by area of expertise, to keep better track of feedback as well as provide useful information in a more organized and powerful way.

---

5   http://www.reedconstructiondata.com/

"I'm a doctoral candidate in business, so to me, Twitter is similar to a strengths, weaknesses, opportunities and threats (SWOT) chart," explains Reale of her Twitter strategy. "If a firm has its 'following' organized and lists them properly, management should be able to discern the SWOT for products, the organization, competitors, customers, prospects; even the industry itself."

By using social media sites like Twitter as a listening tool rather than just blasting promotional messages, Reale discovered that Twitter can help her company reach goals beyond marketing and sales and aide in customer service management as well as product creation and improvement.

"I believe that in business-to-business (B2B), people respond to people. Most companies segment by product or customer base. I thought it might be a good idea to segment by our people in their area of expertise. I wanted to put a human face on the RCD segments," says Reale.

Twitter allows users to easily segment followers and the people they follow through the creation of lists. Some organizations even develop completely different Twitter accounts for each content area of their company to allow for strategic development of different types of customer leads and distribution of more targeted information. By creating diRCDReed is able to have different individuals within RCDshare information that is most valuable to each target audience and therefore create more loyal followings.

Never interrupt — Instead, foster dialogue

The biggest mistake marketers make with social media, regardless of industry, is interrupting rather than contributing to the conversation. By using your own employee resources to add expertise to conversations, you can provide more authentic value to target audiences.

"My twitter feed highlights social media, marketing and business/technology news, with a spotlight on AEC," described Reale of how each employee contributes different content to the segmented Twitter followers. "Another Reed [RCD] employee, Kathy, has CSI and CDT credentials and is a technical writer for building product manufacturers. Kathy tweets a good deal about manufacturing and she follows and talks to manufacturers on her Twitter feed. She understands their pain points, the stuff that keeps them up at night." We'll talk more about how you can engage your employees in social media in Chapter 5.

For A/E companies trying to reach several different target audience groups, segmentation allows the ability to provide specific information that is useful and relevant to the needs of each audience group. The result of this relevant information is that it can, in turn, develop stronger, deeper connections with each audience. Reale believes this type of segmentation will help Reed Construction Data develop better products by listening to feedback and asking questions to the right audiences. And Twitter is not the only social network to benefit from segmentation. Many A/E professionals and firms have set up multiple blogs, each focusing on different topics to appeal to various audiences. You can also set up lists within your Facebook profile so that specific messages will only go out to those "friends" most interested in your company updates. To set up a different list in Facebook, simply click on "Friends", then "Edit Friends." From here, you will see a link that says "Create a List." This will allow you to name the list and add certain Facebook friends to that list.

Top social networks of the design and planning industry

It is important to note that social networks are not just for the young. Internet users between ages 34-44 are dominating the social media space, becoming the fastest adopters of social media use[6]. This audience represents the incoming wave of industry leaders since they will be the 50-year-olds likely running the A/E firms in 10 years. From our conversations with these industry folks, they understand that using social media helps them reach a variety of business goals efficiently, from positioning themselves as thought leaders, to finding new clients, to keeping a pulse on what is happening in the their industry. Social media savvy firms like Ontario, California-based HMC Architects[7] recognize social media as a shift in behavior. "We knew that in order to compete, we had to dive in and stay current with technology and new forms of communication," notes the firm's Los Angeles, California-based Public Relations Manager Nick Bryan. "We're prepping and positioning for the next generation of clients that will expect A/E firms to have a solid presence in their social media networks."

We spoke with professionals in the design and construction industry to understand how they are currently using the top social networking

6   http://royal.pingdom.com/2010/02/16/study-ages-of-social-network-users/
7   http://hmcarchitects.com

channels and what goals and audiences they are reaching by doing so. According to our 2011 survey of A/E and environmental consulting firm professionals, LinkedIn and Facebook are the social networks used most frequently. Use of Twitter, message boards, YouTube and blogs are less common, but a significant number of respondents are planning to launch a blog in the coming months.

In addition to the networks mentioned above, some A/E professionals also mentioned niche networking sites like Archinect.com, Architizer. com, Land8Lounge.com, YourBuilderLink.com and others. Social media happens fast, and new niche networks and blogs arise almost daily. By the time this book goes to press there could be a bigger, faster, better site in place. A great tool to help you stay current with these websites and also monitor the pulse of the online conversation in the A/E industry is Google Alerts. This is a free tool that will email you when your chosen keywords are talked about online. Simply go to google.com/alerts and enter keyword phrases, such as your company name or latest project name, along with your email address to be notified each time anything related to these topics appears online. As professional social media and communications consultants, Google Alerts is an invaluable tool to discover new blogs and smaller, more niche communities that are discussing hot topics where clients would benefit from being heard.

Sometimes what looks like the smallest online community to an outsider can actually have powerful voices developing opinions and dialogue that will eventually spill over to the more popular social networks. Understanding these core audiences, who the key influencers are, what issues are most important to them and how to get your company, project and mission in their good graces can be an invaluable asset. Listening, monitoring and helping to guide dialogue on these niche, smaller sites can help you better understand the thought process behind what motivates your core audiences to support your company and your future projects.

This listening technique can also help you avoid a major PR nightmare on sensitive projects. It allows you to see negative comments coming before the conversations gain leverage in front of major media channels on the bigger social networks.

In addition to helping you discover new places your company should engage, setting up a Google Alert with your own company name as the keyword allows you to be notified anytime anyone online is talking about your company. Being able to listen in to what audiences are saying about you and having a chance to respond is what gives social media such powerful reach. If you are simply using social media to post press releases and company announcements you are missing the point of social networking. Monitoring the online responses to these press releases and announcements is the real power of these tools.

As you dive deeper into social media, you will want to use more advanced social monitoring tools. Companies like Lithium Technologies[8] and Radian 6[9] allow you to track and engage with anyone who is mentioning your company on the social web. Using either of these website tools, simply type in your company name or a project name to track the online news coverage and what people on Facebook, YouTube, Twitter, blogs, or websites are saying about your firm or project. Almost anything that is mentioned on the social web

8   http://www.lithium.com/what-we-do/social-customer-suite/social-media-monitoring
9   radian6.com

will pop up using these listening tools. These social monitoring tools go deeper than Google Alerts as you can actually click on the post from the application and respond to the online discussion in one step.

Social media monitoring tools can also be valuable at helping you keep an eye on your competition. For example, while consulting for Verizon, we used the Scout Labs dashboard (now a part of Lithium's Social Media Monitoring) to compare online sentiment for AT&T to Verizon. Within seconds, a graph showed that Verizon has more mentions and more positive overall sentiment on social media platforms than AT&T.

The network of social media sites is essentially the world's biggest focus group allowing you true insight into what your customers are saying. Additionally and better than the focus group, the social web gives you the real-time ability to respond and add to this discussion. You don't have to be a major company like Verizon to generate an overwhelming amount of social comments from customers that need responses from your company. As an A/E professional, perhaps you are just in the midst of a heated online debate about a new project, which is developing hundreds of posts you'll need to watch. Fortunately, applications like Lithium's Social Media Monitoring not only show you every place your company name is mentioned, but conveniently sorts posts in order of priority, so you can know which posts are most important to respond to. The program determines priorities based on several critical factors, such as how much traffic the web site gets, Google rank, how many people are actively reacting/responding to the post and perhaps most importantly, the online influence of the person who made the comment.

Understanding key influencers within your target audience group

Determining the identity of key influencers within your online social networking circles can be critical to your goals — especially if you tend to carry controversy around specific projects or individuals within your company. How the key influencer in a social circle regards your company can make or break your mission. When this influencer loves your company or project, you can sit back and watch the positive energy flow, but get on their bad side, and you may be confronted with a PR nightmare.

No matter the size, every online community has its loudest voices. And these voices make up only 1% of the total community. But they are a powerful 1%. This select group is essentially the "creator." They are the ones who start conversations and keep the discussions alive over the course of several days or weeks. The creators have a huge influence on the attitudes and energy of the social group.

It may appear that a social network is not active or that no one is listening due to the small percentage of participants actually createing content. As shown in figure 2.3, 10% of a community is what is known as "editors." These members will post and contribute to conversations started by the "creators." They are the ones who will simply "like*" something on Facebook, or contribute a "me too" type blog comment.

1% of community members are creators
10% are editors
89% are just listening

So what are the remaining 89% of the members doing? Listening.

Even though you may think no one is paying attention to your posts and comments, they are. Social media provides a voyeuristic view of what's happening in your online community. For the same reason reality television took off, social media offers a chance for people to listen in, see your ideas and hear what's going on in a fairly anonymous way.

Finding new employees on LinkedIn

LinkedIn provides an ideal way for you to find new employees, vendors and even open yourself up to new customers and projects. In today's online world, more and more people in charge of hiring look to recommendations on LinkedIn before anything else. Of our survey of A/E professionals, 73% are actively using LinkedIn, and more than half are using it to recruit and to connect with vendors, partners or subconsultants.

"I put a lot of weight on referrals received via Twitter and LinkedIn," admits Amy Good, vice president of finance of Lancaster County Timber Frames of Lititz, Pennsylvania. She uses LinkedIn frequently in her company's search for employees, partners or vendors.

Making sure your personal LinkedIn profile is complete, up-to-date and you have quality reviews is a great way to help your profile show up in LinkedIn's professional searches, which helps your target audiences find you.

The primary benefit of LinkedIn is the ability to connect with other people in your industry and for the opportunity to get introduced to their connections, thereby expanding your network of quality business contacts very quickly. Once your profile is up-to-date, LinkedIn will help you easily find your connections by content pulled from your profile, such as past employers and the schools you attended.

But adding a profile and connecting with others in your industry is only a minor part of LinkedIn. There is an extremely targeted, active question and answer community happening behind the scenes in the LinkedIn social network. Not engaging in these discussions is like showing up at an industry tradeshow, event, or conference and not talking to anyone. You did not attend the happy hour afterwards or even the break-out sessions during the event. You just showed up at the registration table and signed in. Maybe you dropped a business card in the fish bowl in hopes someone might notice you and give you a call. You are a LinkedIn wallflower if you are passing up the opportunity to chime in on these discussions.

Only 20% of our survey respondents are using LinkedIn to demonstrate thought leadership or advance the intellectual brand of their firm. Even so, there are an ample number of active AE industry LinkedIn groups. There is a search function at the top of your LinkedIn page where you can input keywords relevant to your industry or research which professional organizations, groups or magazines the other key players in your industry belong to. Join as many as you can realistically keep up with. You'll quickly find that these resources can provide an excellent way to learn from your peers and clients and show off your expertise to the right potential client or partner who is looking for your skills.

Here are some LinkedIn groups we found that are highly active in various A/E circles:

The Urban and Land Institute (ULI)

The American Institute of Architects (AIA) —— national + local chapters

KA Connect

Society for Marketing Professional Services (SMPS)

Landscape Urbanism

LEED Accredited Professional

US Green Build Council

American Planning Association(APA)

Architect

American Society of Landscape Architects (ASLA)

McGraw-Hill Construction

Design Construction Network

Death by Architecture

Urban Design Network

To learn more about or join these groups, log in to your LinkedIn account, select "Groups" and enter these names into the search field. Also consider joining groups your clients may be involved in. Organizations like the Society for College and University Planning (SCUP) and groups like Corporate Real Estate & Facility Management Professionals have large and very active memberships and encourage input from vendors and consultants.

While in LinkedIn some groups are open to anyone who is interested in joining, other groups are created with a particular audience in mind and opt to have a "closed" group. Administrators of these groups only approve new members that fit this demographic. A/E firms are also using LinkedIn as a way of maintaining connections with past employees. These discussion groups are often limited to current and past employees but some firms also allow consultants, subcontractors or partner companies to participate as well.

Can't find an existing LinkedIn group that meets your goals? Start a new one. In Chapter 8, we'll provide tips on how to build and nurture a social media community. We also recommend making the most of your LinkedIn company page and discuss this further in Chapter 3.

Reaching your goals with Twitter

By 2013, nearly 28 million Americans will be tweeting[10]. A/E professionals say tweeting is a great way to monitor what competitors and thought leaders are doing, stay informed of recent articles and

---

10   emarketer.com, February 2011

blog posts relating to a subject of interest and get the inside scoop on what stories the media is researching.

Twitter users follow* people, organizations and companies of interest to receive real-time communications from these companies. Another way of using Twitter is to search for a keyword to sort all the tweets that mention the topic. Spend a little time reading the results and you can pick up on the topic-specific lingo and common hashtags. A hashtag is the # symbol followed by a key term, like #skyscraper or combined shortened terms, like #landarch or acronyms like #AEC. Hashtags are used for more than just listening in on streams to identify influencers in a particular field. They allow conversations among fellow attendees at offline events and conferences and are the organizing element of Twitter events like AIA's monthly chat (#AIAchat) or Balmori Associates'[11] 2009 "Making Public Spaces" Twitter forum that tested the merit of social media — in this case, Twitter — as an aid to a public dialog and debate.

Balmori Associates, the N.Y.-based landscape architecture and urban design firm hosted an in-person discussion of public space in its New York office with 40 Dutch landscape architecture students and their professors. In an interest to open the conversation to participants worldwide, Balmori Associates combined streaming video and Twitter, using the hashtag #mpplaces. The discussion used a Balmori project, the redesign of the public spaces in Balmori's own neighborhood (the Meatpacking District of New York's Greenwich Village) as the focus. The Twitter forum, with internal and external participants, narrowed in on the topics of shared space, urban decorum, context and public spaces' relationship between past and present.

11   http://www.balmori.com

"What I found of greatest value in Twitter was that it allows non-hierarchical comments; it did not become a debate of stars," writes the firm's Principal Diana Balmori in her summary of this discussion[12]. The confines of 140 characters limits intellectual intimidation and as a result generates more input, because everyone relies on simple language to drive home their point. Participants were able to react instantly to the speaker's comments. Balmori continues, "Twitter diminishes the gulf between speaker and audience." Because participants are able to react instantly to shifts in conversation, "it increases participation by making everyone a speaker."

"Originally, I used Twitter to research information on various topics using hashtags," explains Kristin Worley, marketing facilitator of Woolpert, Inc.[13], a national design firm from Charlotte, N.C. "However, I realized how much value Twitter actually provided. I have used the articles and networking I gained through Twitter to guide internal corporate staff in their decision-making processes. Twitter also provides the opportunity for knowledge sharing among individuals, organizations and companies in the industry. Our marketing group has also used it to communicate with others regarding conference events, which is a great way to open more doors to conferences and tradeshows and further extend value to the attendees."

To help you get the most out of Twitter, try using TweetDeck, HootSuite or Sprout Social to organize those you follow into streaming lists. You can also use these sites to set up ongoing keyword and hashtag searches in an easy-to-see-it-all interface. The Twitter

---

12   MAKING PUBLIC PLACES Twitter Forum: What should a public place be? by Diana Balmori + Balmori Associates + Erik de Jong and available for purchase on www.blurb.com.
13   http://www.woolpert.com/

programs mentioned above can also help schedule future tweets, post updates to your other social platforms and monitor your influence and who your top influencers are.

We'll talk more about how you can increase Twitter followers and amplify your efforts in Chapter 3.

Who's on Facebook?

Most professionals in the A/E industry that we interviewed were quick to write off Facebook as a place solely for personal relationships and not for business. However, there are a handful of A/E professionals, primarily in the architecture and design industries, that are creating vibrant Facebook pages with hundreds and even thousands of active followers sharing insightful information, opinions and interesting projects.

Facebook's broad appeal can also be useful in A/E project work. Something that came up several times in our interviews was the fact that architects in particular saw a void in the current social communications with the public. "As an industry, we seem to not provide as much beneficial information to the general public as other industries," said Christian Rogers, principal at Blackmon Architects in Birmingham, Alabama[14]. "I think we could promote ourselves better if we were able to provide information that helps homeowners improve their day-to-day lives."

---

14 http://www.blackmonrogers.com

After all, reaching out to the actual people that will be living in your developments, shopping your town centers, attending your universities and enjoying your parks and landscapes will become a key component to city and public buy-in. Although most city officials we spoke with admitted to sticking with the traditional processes, every person stated that they are hoping to start leveraging social media in the near future. Community stakeholders are already organizing themselves online. Blogs and Facebook groups, like those for the Neighborhood Empowerment Network, encourage and support the grass-roots initiatives in San Francisco, California's neighborhoods. These networks will become a source of information and insight for future developments.

Greg Weykamp, principal of Edgewater Resources in Saint Joseph, Michigan. used Facebook to improve the public's participation in Edgewater's publicly-funded projects. Weykamp explained that more traditional outreach channels such as public meetings, workshops and surveys skewed the perception of the community's opinions in favor of the over 50 age demographic. This group of people typically has more time to go to more meetings since they generally have fewer young children at home, reduced job commitments and more free time. Using Facebook allowed Edgewater Resources[15] to access a wider range of people that more accurately reflected the community residents. For more about how Edgewater Resources and AECOM used Facebook on a project in Decatur, Illinois, read the Decatur Lakefront case study sidebar.

---

15   http://edgewaterconsultants.com/

Decatur Lakefront Case Study

Firm: Edgewater Resources with AECOM

Project: Public engagement for the Nelson Park Master Plan in Decatur, Illinois

Challenge: Traditional public participation techniques were not capturing input from the entire community of Decatur, Illinois.

Like many traditional public meetings, the demographics of the participants were skewed overwhelmingly towards those over age 50, generally empty nesters and with a fairly consistent point of view. This segment of the community was nearly universally opposed to a residential waterfront component of the master plan, with a number of them loudly voicing their opinions to that effect.

In a typical public meeting, the only way to be heard is to stand at a microphone in front of 100 people, state your name and give your opinion with tape recorders and often cameras rolling. There is a small segment of the population who are comfortable standing up and passionately arguing their points in this way. Because many people are uncomfortable speaking in public, while they may be supportive of an idea, they're not willing to stand up and disagree with the naysayers, meaning that those who are comfortable engaging in this way or who are able to attend the meetings often have their point of view over-represented, which leaves out a large population of people from being engaged in the process.

Our client was frustrated by the lack of participation by the wider community, so one of the younger members of their staff suggested using Facebook to reach this demographic.

Objective: To engage community members that were not participating in the planning process.

Strategy: Create a Facebook page to allow dialogue and increase awareness of the project.

A project website was created at the very beginning of the project to document the meetings, announce the schedule and make presentation materials available to the public. As it became clear during the stakeholder interview and initial public meeting process that the younger demographic was not being reached, a meeting was sought with a young professionals group called the 501 Club. The Facebook page was essentially launched during this meeting. It took off with the support of the park district staff and grew very quickly. The Facebook page was further advertised at subsequent public meetings and on the project website.

Within weeks, the Facebook page had hundreds of fans (ultimately more than 1,500) and the debate over the residential component moved to the Facebook discussion thread. The younger demographic was nearly universally in support of this component of the project, as were the local employers. The ultimate task of Edgewater Resources was to listen to the community and with the addition of the Facebook page there was a much more accurate representation of the opinions of the whole community.

Once the conversation moved to Facebook, the naysayers immediately followed. In this forum however, supporters who would never attend a public meeting or speak in front of a crowd were very comfortable voicing their opinions. Very quickly, it became clear that there were many more supporters than naysayers. The discussions were mature, polite and constructive for the most part, and given the forum, not any more anonymous than a public meeting. In this forum, though, the dialogue occurred over a longer period of time, at all hours of the day and night, and in a written format, which means it can be documented exactly as it occurred.

Once the Facebook engagement started, the key element was the quality and civility of the conversation. Ultimately it wasn't about who was for or against this particular issue that made the process successful but that the views of the entire community were being more accurately represented. The most important factor in the success and implementation of any project like this is the support of the public. For Edgewater Resources, the traditional methods would have resulted in a plan that was inconsistent with the goals of two thirds of the community.

Resources:
http://www.facebook.com/decaturslakefront
http:// www.decaturslakefront.com
http://www.edgewaterresources.com/

One reason many businesses are frustrated with Facebook is that after they have spent time building up work relationships on their personal profiles (sometimes under a business name) Facebook is then forcing them to create a Facebook fan page and stop using their profile as a business page. Facebook clearly states in its terms and conditions that profiles are meant for individuals and pages are meant for groups, businesses and organizations. In fact, if you have your business functioning under a profile rather than a fan page, Facebook can shut it down, and all of your "friends" will literally disappear. Trust us! This happened to a client who insisted on using a Facebook profile page rather than fan page.

It's understandable why people don't want to switch over to a fan page from a profile page; it takes time to build up friends, for one. Fortunately, as of April 2011, Facebook added the "Profile to Page Migration" tool that allows you to easily convert your existing profile to a business page and all of your friends to "likes." We suggest you download a backup of your profile before making this transfer as there is no way to convert a page back to a user profile once you engage the tool, and since Facebook profiles function differently than Facebook pages, not all content and information gets carried over. Visit http://www.facebook.com/note.php?note_id=214139221935487 to learn more about backing up your profile page and how to use the page migration tool.

While many A/E company pages on Facebook are mostly "liked" by employees, Balmori Associates only has about 15 professionals on staff,but has attracted more than 800 fans. Pulling content for updates from the firm's established rhythm of publishing and press coverage, the firm created their Facebook page two months in advance of their 2009 Making Public Places event. As the event drew near, the Facebook page and the firm's equally new Twitter account, @Balmorilab, were used to build awareness for the event and invite participants. After the event, coverage from several design publications and blogs attracted new fans and followers interested in learning more about the findings. Fans "like" their posts and the occasional comment is usually met with a friendly Balmori Associates reply.

In the fall of 2010, Diana Balmori released her latest book, A Landscape Manifesto. The audience the firm had attracted via Facebook and Twitter was leveraged for the social media efforts for the book, which included a blog and Facebook fan page. Updates and contributions to the blog in addition to book press, interviews, book readings and even a music playlist that Balmori created were all echoed through the firm's established social channels

Posting the Facebook "like*" widget on your blog posts and web site are obvious ways to encourage people to "like" you and therefore join your fan page. Although Facebook pages are slower to grow and may not give you the direct, measurable impact of LinkedIn, Twitter and a blog, it is still highly recommended to get started now. By 2013, 62% of web users and almost half (47.6%) of the overall U.S. population will be on Facebook[16]. And Facebook users are an active group with 50% logging in every day. In March 2011, Google changed its algorithm to give even more weight to social authority and online reputation. Now the number of "likes" a company has on Facebook directly impacts its overall Google ranking. Read more about Facebook group and fan pages in chapter 3.

---

16   emarketer 2011

The American Institute of Architects (AIA)[17], initially began testing its members' openness to social networking with a LinkedIn group for its members. "Because of its favorable reception and steady growth, we then set up the Facebook group. That, too, was well received. But we began to wonder if perhaps a closed group limits our reach. In 2009 we experimented with a Facebook fan page and Twitter account, both open to all," said Sybil Barnes, AIA's director of social media. "Given the economic challenges the architecture profession is facing, we know that our social channels are, for some, their only means of keeping their professional tie to the AIA."

Getting to know Generation Y (your future employees/clients/vendors)

We believe that as the older executives in the A/E industry retire and the current college generation, which grew up with the Internet, moves into key influential roles in the industry, social media use will only expand. It's important to understand this generation and plan accordingly.

Generation Y, or the Millennials, succeed Generation X and include 60 million people born in the mid 1970s to early 2000s. Many of these are the children of baby boomers, so they are sometimes also referred to as the "echo boomers." This generation spans from young professionals to soon-to-graduate high school students, and most have been exposed to the Internet at an early age. On the whole, they are more computer savvy than any other generation. They are less trusting of corporate media, more likely to ask questions, more likely

---

17   http://www.aia.org/

to share opinions online and they find word-of-mouth an essential part of gathering information. This generation is more likely to Google your company name and see what type of comments come up than to actually visit your company website. Ensuring that the right comments appear during this Google search, to ensure it reflects your brand, mission and goals, is very important.

Why blog?

The best thing about social media is that it is highly flexible. Because you don't need to know any HTML, have graphic skills or know programming languages, it is easier and faster for most people to test, track and monitor than a traditional website. You can quickly gauge the impact of different messaging, and make changes to your strategies and content development directly because of that feedback.

According to our survey of A/E professionals, blogs are one of the least-embraced social web vehicles; only 16% of respondents actively blog. Blogs are an important tool, though. They provide an efficient way for marketers, CEOs, client service representatives and anyone else facing the public in your company to get their messages out fast and efficiently.

We've been seeing firms use blogs as an extension of their website. These can be a work-around to delay a website redesign or to show a more personal side of the company. BKSK[18], an architecture firm in New York with a Flash-based website, created its Tumblr* blog to

---

18   http://bkskarch.tumblr.com/

give the firm online presence that could be seen by iPhones and iPads and to offer a peek at what inspires the firm's creativity.

SWA Group[19], a landscape architecture firm based in Sausalito, California uses their blog, which they refer to as advocacy pages, to give their leading thinkers a place to record their opinions and observations at a particular time. The ongoing quality of blogs — a sequential, date-stamped series of posts — gives the author the freedom to take a stand on an issue because they can always update their position in a later post.

Many firms that do blog use their blog as a social media hub, the origin of the content for all of their other social outlets. One example is previously mentioned HMC Architects. HMC approaches social media as a supplement to its public and media relations program. You can read more about how HMC Architects uses a blog-centered social media strategy to help build their brand and reputation in the case study sidebar.

Like any communications vehicle, the best blogs write for a specific audience and purpose. Christine Morris of Construction Specialties, Inc. is an active consumer of content on the social web. "Subscribing to a variety of blogs allows us to stay updated with the latest industry and market information, participate in discussions and voice opinions. Reading blogs written by well-informed "experts" in any given arena enables us to identify thought leaders that we may want to develop relationships with," explains Morris.

---

19   http://www.swagroup.com/advocacy

HMC Case Study

Firm: HMC Architects, Ontario, California

Example: HMC Architects' blog-based social media strategy

Challenge: Even though HMC was founded in 1940 and has grown to one of the largest architecture practices in California, they were relatively unknown outside of their client roster. Further, the firm was more known amongst their mostly repeat clients for cost-consciousness and client-service than for i design.

Objective: To build public awareness for the firm's design, its staff and its new generation of projects.

Strategy: Leverage social media to publish and promote HMC's projects, content and perspectives.

In 2004, HMC made internal changes to strengthen its design. They recruited key design leaders and made internal shifts toward a more design-forward project approach. As projects that benefitted from this design rigor neared completion, the firm turned its attention to public relations.

In 2009, HMC launched its Twitter account and a Facebook page. With a steady flow of new posts and tweets, the firm had more than 1,200 Twitter followers by the end of the year. But it wasn't until they launched their blog in early 2010 when the firm really started to get noticed.

HMC's social media effort is completely driven by the two-member public relations team. In order to showcase the intellect and technical depth of its staff, the public relations team develops content with each practice area. To supplement this proactive effort, the firm launched an internal blog shortly after its external blog came online. HMC's internal blog serves many of the same needs as a traditional intranet — sharing company news, events and celebrating accomplishments — but the alternate agenda is to get employees to join the conversation and contribute their point of view. At first, this required a lot of in-person cajoling from the public relations department but eventually new ideas, posts and feedback were mostly voluntary. As a result, HMC's public relations team pulls many ideas for its external blog, articles or thought pieces just by listening to the internal blog discussions. Sometimes an internal post can be posted on the public blog as-is.

Today, HMC's external blog serves as the hub for all the firm's social media activities. Each practice area (e.g., health care, Pre K-12, higher education, etc.), initiative (e.g., high performance architecture, patient-centered design) and post type (e.g., opinions, awards) is represented through the blog categories so that readers can quickly sort the content by the subject area of interest.

Blog post topics are then used as content for HMC's Twitter and Facebook accounts and, when applicable, a link is sent to relevant journalists and bloggers. Even though it's possible to automate these, HMC tailors the tweet and Facebook posts for each network. By including a link to the blog post in tweets and Facebook updates, HMC conveys the core message and entices readers to click through to the blog to read more. This approach actually makes the other outlets more effective. The click-through rate of HMC's tweets increased 300% one year after the blog was launched.

Lesson: While HMC's blog content tries to balance its own work with useful information and opinions, their close watch of the site's analytics reveal that posts based on a strong opinion prove to be the most successful. For example, one of the firm's senior project designers posted his response to French architect Francois Roche's very public cancelation of a scheduled speech at the independent architecture SCI-Arc in Los Angeles, California. Roche's cancellation letter found its way onto several sites such as The Architect's Newspaper blog (blog. archpaper.com), Archinect (archinect.com) and Architizer (www.architizer.com) and on Facebook and LinkedIn groups like Death By Architecture. By weighing in on this public discussion, HMC generated more blog traffic with this single post than the blog receives in a normal month.

Results: HMC's combination of viewpoints and projects keeps readers returning. As a result, they have garnered coverage in both online and print from the likes of ArchDaily, Architect's Newspaper, Architect Magazine, Architectural Record, Engineering News Record, Archinect, Interior Design and Contract Magazine.

Resources:
http://blog.hmcarchitects.com/   http://hmcarchitects.com
http://www.facebook.com/HMCArchitects   @HMCArchitects

The Green Compliance Plus blog by Mark English Architects (MEA)[20] in San Francsico, California is a great example. MEA primarily designs homes and entertainment spaces, but the firm also works for other architects to calculate buildings' energy efficiency to comply with California's Title 24 standards. MEA started marketing these services through a PDF email, but when that didn't deliver the results expected they transitioned this content onto a Wordpress platform. Before launching the blog, "we had 15–20 clients on the energy compliance side of the business, without any active marketing. The goal was to get to several hundred clients using social media," explained Mark English in an interview on the PhoneWorks blog[21].

Blog strategies only work if the content is good. Instead of looking at this blog as a showpiece for the firm's services, Green Compliance Plus focuses on what the readers' are interested in. Each post is high quality and original content — not a repost from another source. The posts spotlight other companies through interviews with green product manufacturers, builders and other architects and MEA client project case studies. The blog also offers commentary and discussions on compliance and green current events, "how to's" and calculation tips — really useful stuff for MEA's target audience.

But how does MEA's content development strategy help find their targeted audience? According to Morris "We have also found that Twitter helps us find topical news stories, articles and blog posts that are relevant to our industry. This has played a critical role in helping us, especially our sales team, stay current with what's going on in the market at any given time."

---

20 http://greencomplianceplus.markenglisharchitects.com/
21 http://www.sales20book.com/wp/wp-content/uploads/2010/07/EnglishInterview_FINAL_forWeb_071210.pdf

As a result of frequent posts focused on compliance topics, Green Compliance Plus has become a credible resource for architects. Each post is automatically tweeted to @MarkEnglishArch's followers. Twitter provides 20-25% of the blog's readership and drives new followers of 100-120 each week.

Often, the interview subjects add a link to their Green Compliance Plus story on their own website and social networks. The combination of the blog's stream of new content, incoming links from other sites and sources, and a constant focus on the green compliance topic has pushed Green Compliance Plus to the top of search engine results for green keywords and even their interview subjects' names and firms. Over the course of his first year blogging, MEA tripled their compliance business.

Now that you have found your target audiences and have discovered a good mix of social tools to reach them, you need to amplify those efforts. In the next chapter, we'll show you how you can increase your followers, fans, traffic and longevity of your online messaging.

Chapter 3
Amplifying your Communication Efforts

So you've set up your company Twitter, launched the Facebook fan page, updated your LinkedIn profile and started a blog. Now what? How do you attract the attention of friends, followers and fans — and keep them interested enough to not only listen but also share your message with their friends, followers and fans?

Before we dive into the specific tricks and strategies that will help you reach your business goals via Twitter, YouTube, Facebook or other social sites, we want to stress that no matter which social tool you use, your messaging should be centered around encouraging engagement. Social networking is about making a connection with your online friends, fans and followers. It is about encouraging them to react, post opinions and engage. Social media is not all about you.

It is not about the latest press release your PR consultant posted on the newswire this morning or the big project you just landed last week. It is, however, about how these bits of information may affect the lives, projects and companies of your audiences. The information you post should be interesting, relevant, timely and emotionally charged to entice your audience to react in some way, whether it is posting a comment, expanding on the idea, sharing that information with others or taking the desired business action you intended when you made the post.

Practice patience when starting your social media campaign

As you try the tricks and strategies outlined in this chapter, keep in mind that developing a successful social media presence takes time and patience. Although you may not feel the immediate results as quickly as you could through a simple pay-per-click campaign*, social media outreach, when positioned correctly, will outlast any paid advertisement. In fact, each blog post, comment and tweet is still accessible by search engines long after your pay-per-click or other advertising campaigns have expired.

When you have something important to share or an opinion that sparks others to react, your message can grow exponentially. A company that steps outside of the box to post original commentary or even something entertaining or humorous will win out over the corporate blogger who continues to push out standard press releases and mission statements without creating an environment where people feel comfortable sharing or reacting.

Laura Davis and Larry Paschall, principals of HPD Architecture LLC[1] in Dallas, Texas say that engaging in social media is imperative to their firm's survival as a business. They decided to use social media to help HPD stand out from other architectural firms with the goal of bringing in work. However, as they entered the social media space, they started to see that building a solid online social network takes time and patience.

"We knew we could not expect to appear on social media outlets and have new clients start walking through our door, just as you cannot expect business to come to you just because you design a website or have a phone number," states Davis.

Like many other successful social media users in the A/E industries, Davis and Paschall have discovered that it is not one specific tool that helps them discover and gain new projects and clients, but a combination of them. HPD uses a combination of blogging, Twitter, LinkedIn, Facebook and Meetup (which we'll talk more about later in the chapter) to reach their business goals of building awareness and establishing credibility as "talented, friendly and trustworthy architects in the Dallas area."

"Our blog has been essential in helping move our ranking up within Google. However, a blog does not stand alone and utilizing each social media tool in a combined effort has been the key ingredient in creating the results we have seen", says Paschall. "We have not seen clients come to us because we are on Twitter. But what we have seen are opportunities to participate in webinars for marketing companies,

---

1   http://www.hpdarch.com

opportunities to speak at professional conferences, and opportunities to be a valued resource for a variety of companies."

Participate unselfishly

As you begin to set up your own social media strategy, spend part of your time on the social networks unselfishly. In other words, spread your wisdom on Quora, LinkedIn or blogs to help others. Comment on other people's blogs, share your colleague's content, "like" other people's fan pages, and retweet other people's words. However, choose ways to be unselfish that are also related to your industry and overall business goals. While it is important to share information and other people's content, consistency in your own messaging will empower your social media campaign. Therefore, choose topics to share and comment on that are related to your own expertise so you don't confuse your existing fans and followers. After all, anywhere you post online has the potential to be found via search engines by potential clients.

"The A/E industry should understand how social media really works," says Paschall. "A lot of companies will simply view social media tools as a means to promote and talk about themselves and their projects or products. Unfortunately, that is the quickest way to have their listeners tune out. People that follow a company on social media are looking for useful, relevant information." Paschall says.

In addition to participating unselfishly, it is important to be genuine. By engaging on a few of these networks you can use them to tap into your influencers and drive attention to your content. Tools like

Tweetdeck and Hootsuite make it easy to sync all your accounts, but beware of robotically posting the exact same update to Twitter, Facebook, LinkedIn and so on. Each network has a different culture. To the people who follow you on more than one site, your repetitive messages are the equivalent of spam. "Each time we [blog], we run through a process of social promotion where we share via Facebook, Twitter, Digg and StumbleUpon," says Scott Doyon, principal and director of marketing of PlaceMakers, LLC. "We also promote [the blog post] on Listservs where growth, development, environmental and community-building issues are discussed." For an in depth look at how PlaceMakers promotes their posts in order to drive readership and the thinking that underlies this strategy, read their case study side bar. As you truly engage on these social spaces, you will realize that there is a different way to communicate with each of these groups. Take your different audiences into account and communicate with them the way they want to interact.

Finally, once you post something online, don't abandon it. Listen and react thoughtfully to any feedback you get. Take time to reply to direct tweets and blog comments with a thoughtful response that will keep conversations going, rather than a quick "thanks for the comment!"

PlaceMakers Case Study

"Social media has become the engine that drives our readership."

Attracting Readership: Writing and posting a solid blog post is not enough. People still have to find it. PlaceMakers; blog is written for a broad audience, so they use social media to share each post beyond RSS subscribers. Scott Doyan shares their promotion protocol.

Testimonial: Scott Doyan, Atlanta, Georgia-based principal at PlaceMakers, a multidisciplinary, new economy planning firm with seven principals located in seven different cities across the U.S. and Canada, explains the firm's social promotion process that it uses to attract readers to its "PlaceShakers and NewsMakers" blog posts.

Objective: To reach people in a lot of different places without imposing ourselves on them.

We see place making through a pretty wide lens. We're building relationships with environmentalists, developers, city boosters, bike and pedestrian advocates, foodies and all kinds of other folks who care about community improvement.

When we write a blog post, we try to put the broad-based interests of our audience at the center, which can generate comments where we might get a real conversation going. Or, it might not. It's hit or miss, just like life.

The traditional approach to marketing has always been to cut through all the clutter, get in the face of your target audience and have something of value to offer. It's not a conversation. It's a pitch. Your goal is to sell something and those who aren't interested tend to simply endure it because they know that's what you're doing.

Social media, however, is about conversations and relationships and that requires far greater sensitivity.

Strategy: To put ourselves out there and try to be useful.

Typically, one of [the principals] will write once a week. We do this not to promote our work (we rarely, if ever, discuss our projects) but to advance the larger community-building/smart growth conversation and to raise our individual profiles within that conversation.

Social media has become the engine that drives our readership because it's so efficient at breaking us out of our vocational silo of urban design practitioners and connecting with all kinds of like-minded groups with different agendas but similar end goals.

When we launch a new blog post, the first thing we do is to create a bit.ly link, instead of letting the page buttons create them for us. This lets us watch flow as we post to various places, and gauge the relative speed and interest. Using that link, we create a short description of the post, that may only be two sentences, and:

  1. Digg it.

  2. Bookmark it on Delicious , providing a description, tagged with keywords, in the notes field.

  3. Fave it on Technorati.

4. Recommend it on StumbleUpon.

5. Tweet it on Twitter and on Twibe

6. Go to email and create a new email to post@(NameOfYourPage).com. Paste the description and bit.ly link into the email. Send it to Posterous, where it posts as another, shorter blog.

7. Post to our various Facebook pages or any Facebook event page where it's applicable.

8. Share as an update on LinkedIn.

9. Add the title of the blog and its hyperlink to the signature of our emails, which is subsequently replaced by each new blog post.

10. Post to the listservs to which we belong, most of which are related to urbanism, community or architecture.

11. Over time, extract key points, and Twitter/Twibe them again, or write a note of them on StumbleUpon.

12. Write a slightly longer description, tying into any associated news articles and submit for entry to Planetizen.com, Land8Lounge.com and SustainableCitiesCollective.com, which are planning-related news blogs.

placemakers social media flow chart

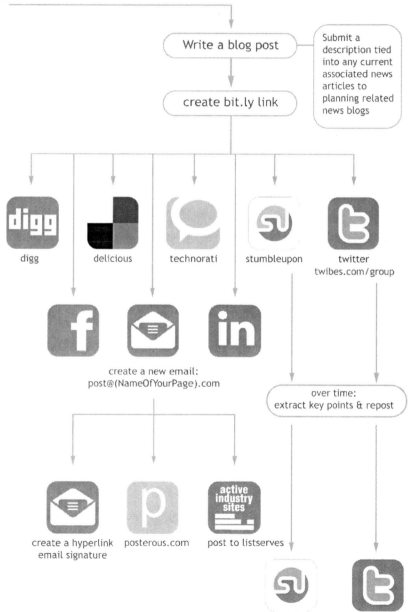

Write a blog post

Submit a description tied into any current associated news articles to planning related news blogs

create bit.ly link

digg

delicious

technorati

stumbleupon

twitter
twibes.com/group

create a new email:
post@(NameOfYourPage).com

over time:
extract key points & repost

create a hyperlink
email signature

posterous.com

active industry sites

post to listserves

So sure, we promote things we're writing or doing sometimes but we don't make that our sole contribution to the conversation. We also promote things other people are doing. Or illustrate connections between seemingly disparate events. Or add a little levity.

Of course, there are still the more basic rules of etiquette.

- Don't inundate your mailing list or contacts with content.
- Be respectful of people's time.
- Don't comment on other people's blog posts with links to your own stuff.
- If you tweet, don't be solely self-promotional.
- Serve other people's interests, not just your own.

Additional Resources:

placeshakers.wordpress.com   www.placemakers.com

www.digg.com   www.delicious.com

www.technorati.com   www.stumbleupon.com

www.twibes.com/group/cityplanners   www.posterous.com

Make the most of your offline assets

Subject-matter experts are often drawn to traditional tactics for promoting their ideas and innovations, such as publishing and speaking publicly, as a means of advancing their practice and their profession. Professional service firms that see the upside of thought leadership and knowledge sharing as a way to build a highly skilled team and the company's reputation support and encourage these efforts. Social media's culture of sharing is a natural fit.

Perhaps you recently made a presentation to your local chapter of the American Society of Civil Engineers ASCE, this presentation could drive the content of your next blog post — or two. Consider expanding on a couple of your points or posting an edited video of the presentation. You can extend this reach even further by tapping into affiliates and partnerships. Link back to your chapter's website or blog and mention the chapter's @name when you tweet about it. Follow your social promotions up with a phone call (After all, these relationships aren't limited to digital discourse.) or email to your ASCE chapter contact to ask if they would link to your blog post from theirs or to "like" your mention of it on your Facebook page or to retweet your tweet.

We recently helped HMC Architects promote a white paper they had co-authored with Planetree[2], a non-profit organization that advocates for hospitals to adopt a holistic patient-centered model. "Design and the Bottom-Line" is a 21-page presentation of the benefits of incremental patient-centered design changes. Instead of just publishing the whitepaper and encouraging people to download and read it in its entirety, they created a 10-part blog series that expands on individual topics discussed in the paper — effectively extending the longevity of the message by 10 weeks.

HMC also began listening in on patient-centered and healthcare tweets and discussion threads on various LinkedIn groups to look for opportunities to share their patient-centered-design insights. When

---

2 http://www.planetree.org/

appropriate, HMC directed people to the whitepaper or to a particular blog post.

HMC's partnership with Planetree multiplied their efforts by tapping into the non-profit's communications network. Planetree also published the white paper on their website and promoted it in their own communications vehicles including an email newsletter that goes to anyone who opts in to receive it and posted it in their members-only community. Planetree published a summary article in their monthly magazine Planetalk, and of course included it in Planetree's tweets, LinkedIn group discussion and Facebook page. This campaign was designed to not only position the authors, as well as HMC and Planetree, as a source of deep knowledge on this topic but also to strengthen the relationship between the two organizations. Partnering with another organization effectively extends the reach of the joint message in a targeted way and introduces the brands to the other's network.

Similarly, HPD realized the depth of their social network relationships would only benefit from taking the discussions offline. So, the firm created their own networking event, The Architecture Happy Hour, and leveraged the social network Meetup to drive attendance. Meetup is a global network of local groups with more than 7 million members in 45,000 cities. HPD uses it as a resource to find existing networking groups that fit their business and as a way to manage and promote their own. "By hosting and organizing the group, we

HMC's social media audience covers a diverse spectrum of interests related to the firm's specialties. When HMC co-authored a whitepaper about healthcare with Planetree, their individual social networks collided and expanded. Together, HMC and Planetree have found a niche group interested in the intersection between architecture and healthcare.

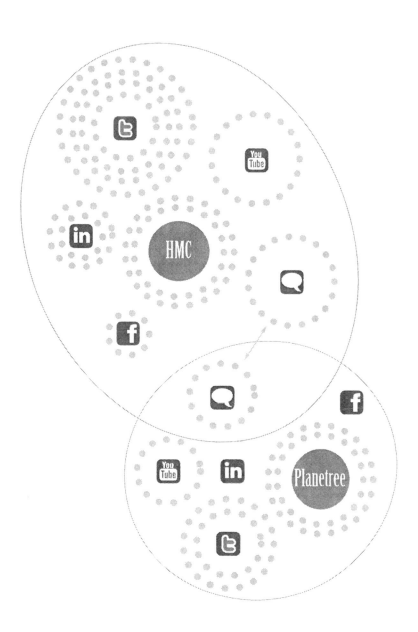

connect people in the A/E community with synergy partners to whom they might not otherwise be introduced," says Paschall. "We also hope having the happy hour group will encourage other people in the community to start networking and start understanding that there is a value in building a business referral network."

How often should you tweet, post, comment...?

90%
unsubscribe

posts are too frequent

posts are irrelevant

boring communications

90% of consumers unsubscribe, "unlike"* or stop following companies because of too frequent, irrelevant or boring communications[3]. In other words, the content of your messages is just as important as how often you push those messages out. Studies have shown that one update on Facebook per day is optimal, while you can tweet up to seven times per day on Twitter (as long as they are spread out throughout the day and not in quick successionToo many updates is the quickest way to loose fans, followers and friends.

According to the Digital Insights package on "Attentionomics"[4] created by global PR firm Edelman and released by Syomos, the massive growth of social media makes it harder for a firm's message to stand out. For example, of the more than 110 million tweets per

3   "The Social Break-Up," 2011, ExactTarget.com
4   http://www.slideshare.net/EdelmanDigital/attentionomics-captivating-attention-in-the-age-of-content-decay

day on Twitter, the report says that "each tweet decays almost as soon as it is released." According to Syomos, "92% of all retweets (and 97% of replies) happen within the first 60 minutes."

The same report discovered that in general, most Facebook users log in at the top and bottom of each hour. Similar studies have found that first thing in the morning, at lunch time and in the late afternoon are the most active times on Facebook. This means that your post must gain some momentum (comments/likes) to keep it at the top of your fans' newsfeedbefore and during these times. Keep in mind, though, that the "time of day" statistics are for the general population of Twitter and Facebook and not broken down by specific audience. Despite that fact, these statistics still serve as a great starting point and guideline to when you should start posting; however, as you develop a core following of your target audience, you may find a different time of day that is best to post. There are new social media monitoring tools like Timely by FlowTown[5], that will help you track reaction to your tweets and posts by time of day so you can understand

5   www.flowtown.com, creator of small business marketing tools

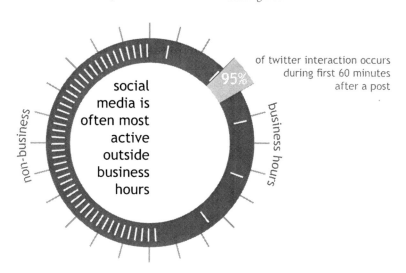

social media is often most active outside business hours

non-business

business hours

95% of twitter interaction occurs during first 60 minutes after a post

what timeline works best for your company and goals. (Turn to Chapter 7 for more details on how you can track, test and monitor timing for maximum benefit.)

Consider the benefit social media plays in your Google ranking

Don't get discouraged if you haven't had time to write a new blog post this week or that your latest tweet is already obsolete just seconds after you posted it. Even if you don't get an immediate reaction from a post you've made, Google can still keep it alive long after you've moved on to the next message. Social media now plays an important role in helping you stay at the top of search engines. Popular search engines like Google aim to provide users with the most relevant and up-to-date information. Therefore Google now indexes and displays tweets, videos on YouTube — which Google now owns — and blog posts (sometimes even before your website). For more detailed information about search engine optimization (SEO)strategies, you can pick up a copy of co-author Holly Berkley's "Marketing in the New Media" or "Low Budget Online Marketing for Small Business."[6] For the purposes of social media search engine optimization, incorporating keywords into your posts is vital to increasing the longevity of your social media efforts. Emissions Compliance

Here are a few tips to help your search engines find your social media efforts:

>> Incorporate keywords into the title of your blog.

---

6   http://www.berkweb.com

>> When blogging, never link back to your website with a "click here." Instead, use your keywords in the link. For example, "learn more about our Dallas interior architecture projects." This give the keyword term "Dallas interior architecture" more weight and helps your website's ranking.

>> Don't use a Facebook profile for your business. These profile pages are password protected and therefore any text beyond the public descriptions on the information page is not visible to search engines. Instead, set up a cause, group or fan page for your business. (Information about converting your Facebook profile to a Facebook page was briefly mentioned in Chapter 2 and will be covered more –in-depth later in this chapter.) In addition, consider your keywords when you select the name of your Facebook page.

>> Whenever possible, always provide a link back to your website or blog (but remember the second bullet point about how to link back!). For example, use your website address in your signature when you post a blog comment. The more incoming links you have to your web site, the better your search ranking.

>> When posting a video on YouTube, take the time to list keywords in the description, as well as use a keyword-friendly title.

>> When using Twitter, use your keywords in your profile bio, and as often as possible in your tweets.

>> Finally, don't over-optimize your titles and posts. "Keyword stuffing" can not only affect your ranking in the exact opposite way, but also make your customers less likely to actually read it. There is a

Keys for Search Engine Optimization:

Include keywords in blog title

Hyperlinc keywords instead of using "click here"

Include links back to your site whenever possible

Facebook: set up a "cause", "group" or "fan page"

YouTube Posts: list keywords in the description and title

Twitter: use keywords in your profile bio and in tweets

⚠ Keyword stuffing can negatively affect search engine rankings and turns off readers. Practice moderation. ⚠

fine balance between creating interesting, reader-friendly content and incorporating search-friendly phrases and keywords.

A look at amplification Strategies by social network

Below is list of top social networks used by the A/E industry today. We've outlined strategies for amplifying your communications on each network.

 Facebook

Facebook is proving to be an excellent way for designers and planners to gain feedback and engage with local communities regarding projects. AECOM[7] is just one of the A/E companies using a Facebook page to gather informal feedback on projects. Yanna Badet, a San Francisco, California-based environmental planner and public involvement specialist for AECOM explained that Facebook provides a way to target a younger audience and to reach out to their friends and neighbors who may be affected by a project.

"I think social media messages needs to be properly targeted. They should be locally applicable, emotionally valuable or useful to the intended audience. A funny or creative picture will be viewed, liked and shared more than plain text," says Badet.

Badet also says that targeted social media and relevant messaging can be difficult for large firms if they try to reach out too generally. Instead, these firms should focus on a specific project. "Tying the social media effort to specific projects and tangible products can help make it a real thing to "like"… The closer a project is to my backyard, the more I will care to join the conversation."

Converting Facebook profile to fan page

According to Facebook's terms of service, "Profiles represent individuals and must be held under an individual name, while pages allow for an organization, business, celebrity, or band to maintain a professional presence on Facebook." A Facebook fan page is designed to become the official Facebook marketing presence for a business, but a business can also set up group or community pages for specific projects or discussions among a smaller collection of users. While fan

---

7   http://www.aecom.com

pages are viewable by everyone on the Internet, groups and community pages can be set up to be private or invitation only. This makes them a good option for internal communications between employees or regarding specific projects or client groups.

Especially in the design industry, a large number of A/E firms are sole proprietors or a firm with less than 24 employees. If you've already built up a lot of friends on your Facebook profile, it's tempting to ignore the rules and use your personal site for business. However, Facebook has the right to shut down a profile that is being used by a business, and if that happens your connection to your Facebook friends will vanish with it and they will all need to be re-added if you start a new profile or page. There are advantages to having a Facebook page instead of a profile. One is the ability for search engines to find it and the other is access to Facebook's analytic tool, Facebook Insights. (More about Insights in Chapter 7.) With a Facebook page, you will also have access to the latest promotional tools, such as like buttons. You also have unlimited growth potential since Facebook doesn't limit the number of fans for a page. Conversely, a Facebook profile is limited to 5,000 friends. See Chapter 2 for more on converting your profile page to a fan page.

Another way to get fans to like your new page is by setting up a Facebook ad. These ads are extremely cost effective for the design and planning industries, costing only a few cents per click. You can target your Facebook ad to promote your new fan page to anyone on Facebook by geographic location, occupation, interests, ages and other key attributes. But keep in mind the more general you make your ad, the more expensive it will be. Or, you can simply create an ad that will only appear to your existing Facebook friends. As your friends begin to like your new page, friends of friends will see that their friend "likes" it in their news feed which brings more credibility to your ad.

1-800-Flowers encourage customers to like their Facebook page by offering immediate discount codes. Other companies have similar promotions. Although coupon codes and sweepstakes might not typically work for design and planning firms, a little incentive can help increase your fan base. Try encouraging likes by giving away a white paper or access to some research or article written by one of your company thought leaders. Offer value to your users.

Regarding the content of your Facebook posts, topics that do best on Facebook are those that make you appear friendly and thoughtful. For example, encourage others to join social causes or charities and also use humor in your posts. Tell stories, use emotion and keep conversations as genuine as possible. Even though your page is business-related keep in mind that people still do business with people — especially in professional services. And don't be afraid to ask people to like you on Facebook. According to Journalistics[8], a blog that covers PR and journalism, Facebook reported in 2010 that journalists who asked readers to like an article the user just read, had two to three times the activity of journalists who did not ask.

Design and planning are visual professions, therefore you should use interesting and thought-provoking imagery to attract attention and get conversations started. Whenever possible, use a photograph, graphic or video of some sort when posting to Facebook. This will naturally attract more eyes to your message. In fact, studies have

---

8 blog.journalistics.com

found that Facebook posts containing an image will get 12 times the engagement compared to those without a picture. Also, consider an interesting profile picture that will help your posts and comments standout in your fans' newsfeeds.

Take advantage of Facebook's interactive applications such as polls and questions — if they relate to your business and would be of value to your fans. Real estate developer Project^ gained most of their more than 800 fans from a simple competition using the poll feature on their Facebook page. Read the Courtside Case Study sidebar for more information about how Project^ used Facebook to encourage tours and sign leases for an off-campus student housing community next to the University of Oregon.

Courtside Case Study

Firm: Project^, Portland, Ore, www.projectpdx.com

Project: Growing a Facebook fanbase for the Courtside property

Challenge: When Facebook is your marketing channel, organic growth is not always fast enough. The Portland, Oregon real estate developer Project^ explains how Facebook's interactive applications helped them quickly grow more than 600 targeted fans.

During the spring 2010 semester, Project^ was in the midst of constructing Courtside, a new off-campus student housing development across the street from what is now the Matthew

Knight Arena on the University of Oregon campus in Eugene. With construction for the arena and Courtside happening simultaneously, there was little awareness of the new property or what this area of town would be.

The 176-bed Courtside development was scheduled to be completed in September 2010, just in time for the fall semester. The spring semester (during Courtside's construction) is the time when most of the leases for the upcoming fall semester are signed. Courtside needed to direct all interested lease signers to the website because there were no model units available to walk-through during this time.

Objective: To sign enough leases to reach a 95% occupancy-rate before the fall semester.

Strategy: Using Facebook as one of the many marketing tools, Project^ ran ads and interactive promotions to create curiosity and interest in learning more about the development. The first step toward attracting future tenants was to get students to click-through to the Courtside website and take a virtual of property. Getting students to like the page was also important to maintain interest through periodic promotions and updates on the construction.

Project^'s most successful promotion was a contest titled "The $1,000 Club Contest." With the help of San Diego, California-based ad agency Farm they put post cards in the mailbox of every on-campus student organization and emailed each club president to ask what their organization would do with a $1,000 donation. Courtside's Facebook page fans would vote on the submittals and select which club would get the prize. "We wanted this to be more than a contest," says Project^ Partner Anyeley Hallova. "We wanted this to help us create a sense of community and attract people who wanted to be a part of a community. By using student organizations we would be reaching groups of students that already shared a common interest." Since students had to like the Courtside page to vote, the club presidents asked their members to become Courtside fans so that they could vote for their club. The vote was held using Facebook's Questions feature and the contest generated more than 600 fans.

Lesson: The collective marketing efforts resulted in more than 80% of the beds leased by fall 2010. While this wasn't the 95% target, Project^ was still pleased with the results. The contest promotion generated likes from a broad sample of students and many click-throughs to the website — Facebook was consistently in the top four of website referrals — but obviously not all of the fans were interested in signing a lease. However, this broad fan base paid off again as the second Project^ property in the Arena District, Skybox, was being built.

The new property has 50% more beds, and benefits from a better awareness of the property's quality and the added foot traffic from the now completed Matthew Knight Arena. Instead of investing in a large campaign as they did with Courtside, Project^ was able to use the Courtside Facebook page to notify people about the new Skybox property and Skybox Facebook page. With a more grass roots approach, the Skybox page has more than 125 likes — a more accurate pool of interested lease signers. With Skybox opening in September for the fall 2011 semester, they are tracking to hit the same 80% occupancy by the time classes start in 2011.

Going forward: Project^ now uses the Facebook pages for both properties to communicate directly with tenants and students considering signing a lease in ways that encourage a stronger sense of community within the property. For example, Project^ uses the Facebook Questions feature to let residents discuss on the communal items available to everyone such as music preferences for common areas, magazines subscriptions, board games and which products they should stock in the vending machines. Personal referrals are the top way for getting new leases and these often happen on Facebook, so it continues to be an important place to for Project^ to connect with future tenants.

Resources:
http://www.projectpdx.com
www.facebookcom/livecourtside
www.livecourtside.com
www.liveskybox.com
www.facebook.com/liveskybox
www.livearenadistrict.comwww.farmsd.com

Finally, take advantage of the news feed. This is where most Facebook users get their content. You want your post to stay on each user's news feed for as long as possible, to generate the most exposure.

Fortunately for small businesses, Facebook's news feed algorithm doesn't use how many fans or friends you have to decide whose post stays on top longest. Rather, posts are prioritized by three things: how recent the post was made, how recently a user interacted with it, and how many likes the post received. Therefore, encouraging comments by asking questions and keeping the conversation active is beneficial to the longevity of the post.

 LinkedIn

As mentioned earlier in this book, participation on LinkedIn means doing more than just setting up a profile and uploading your resume. This applies to both personal and company LinkedIn pages. As of March 2011, more than 90 million LinkedIn members have set up a company LinkedIn page to promote their business. Even if you haven't proactively created an account for your business, there may already be one on LinkedIn. This is because LinkedIn's business directory pulls basic company information (such as number of employees and history) from content collected through its partnership with BusinessWeek. That means that when you view a personal LinkedIn profile, the name of the companies referenced in that profile usually links to a company page.

LinkedIn uses member information to supplement the basic facts and as a result the bulk of the data on company pages is derived directly from member profiles who indicate themselves as an employee. This includes statistics like new hires and recent activity (based on recently added and modified affiliations with the company) or comparative charts between the company and an average of its competitors.

A/E firms that take control of their LinkedIn company page have found another opportunity to drive home their brand personality, showcase their portfolio and validate their work and expertise. Pages allow users to add things such as the company logo, description, website address, Twitter handle, RSS feed and even embed YouTube videos or a news module that displays recent headlines of articles that include your firm. Like other social channels, LinkedIn also has its own set of analytics for monitoring the effectiveness of your page. With a little more effort you can connect your blog and your Twitter feed to your page or even upgrade your account for a monthly fee of about $195 to allow you to post job listings.

As you set up your company page, take the time to fill out the "Services" section. By providing a lot of keyword friendly information here, it will be easier for potential customers, employees and subconsultants to find you. It's also a good idea to solicit recommendations from your clients. Overall, the more complete your profile is, the better it will serve you.

If you've finished setting up your company page, click on the "Promote my company" link. LinkedIn continues to update this section with tools and targeted ad buy opportunities to help you promote your company page.

In professional services, clients are drawn to your firm because of you or your employees and LinkedIn is an excellent place for relationships to be sustained and grown. That is why it is so important to make sure that in addition to your company page that your personal profile is as complete as possible. Also, since LinkedIn pulls information from member pages, the company page will not accurately reflect the current state of your firm if a good percentage of your staff doesn't participate. Therefore you should encourage employees to participate on LinkedIn.

For your personal LinkedIn profile, consider the best keyword phrases that you want to be known for and use these same phrases throughout your profile and bio when appropriate. This will help people better find you through LinkedIn's search. Your professional headline is perhaps the most important piece of your profile. This is what people will see first when they are searching for someone with your skills. By default, your profile headline will be your most recent position or job title. However, you can manually change this to whatever you want. Adding credentials such as AIA, ASLA, LEED, AP, to your title will give a more complete impression of your skills. If your potential clients might not be familiar with the industry acronyms, take time to craft a statement that will not only help you stand out but also describes your strengths while using your keyword phrases. Here are a few strong headline examples we found:

"Casino Construction Project Manager and Operations Consultant"

"Principal and Director of Design, Author, Architect, Urban and Regional Designer, Industrial Designer"

"Environmental & Sustainability Planner, Environmental Compliance/Permitting Consultant, Interagency Liaison & PI Facilitator"

Also, be sure your LinkedIn URL includes your name. This will help people better find you online. Your LinkedIn URL should look resemble http://linkedin.com/in/yourname. In most cases you will need to manually set this up. Simply log in to your profile and scroll down to where your "Public Profile URL" is listed. Click the "edit" button to enter your name. If you have a common name, one that is already taken, you may need to add middle initial or perhaps a period between the first and last name.

Be sure to take a look at the list of LinkedIn applications. LinkedIn frequently adds new ones to help you further promote your profile and messages. Start with using the applications that connect with your other social accounts like Twitter and WordPress. Using these applications will help you easily integrate your most recent blog post into your LinkedIn profile and out to your LinkedIn connections. It's also common for people to connect their Twitter account to their LinkedIn profile. If you opt to do this, keep in mind that this is a professional audience and each tweet will be broadcast to your connections. Chatty tweets between you and another individual or off-topic and personal tweets are noise in the LinkedIn setting. If you are a frequent tweeter (more than 3 times daily), even relevant tweets may get tiresome to your connections when they dominate their LinkedIn update stream.

A reminder to look into LinkedIn groups related to your industry, like we discussed in Chapter 2. Interacting within these groups will help your company stand out among your target audiences. The more you show off your expertise in a group by providing valuable information, the more users will see you as a trusted expert — which reflects positively on your firm as well. This will help build both your company's and your personal online brand.

 **Twitter**

First of all, don't get caught up in the numbers on Twitter. There are paid services where you can gain hundreds to thousands of twitter followers. However, as a design or construction professional, your goal should not be about how many Twitter followers you have, but who those followers are. Find other professionals and firms with the job title, expertise or interest you want to target by searching for keywords or hashtags* related to your industry, such as #LEED, #designbuild, #BIM, #SMPS.

Once you have your list of followers, an easy way to get a specific users' attention is to retweet them, referred to as RT in the actual tweet, or call attention to them using their @name. If expanding your Twitter influence is part of your social media strategy, commit to spending a few minutes each week to retweeting someone. Choose someone with a list of followers that represent your target audience. Make sure to add your own comment or perspective in front of the retweeted message to show a bit of your own personality and perspective. If you are lucky, they may retweet your next post to their followers.

You can also reach out to a Twitter follower privately with a direct message, indicated as DM in your tweet. To keep people from abusing this, direct messages are only available between users who follow each other. You can send a follower a direct message, but if you don't follow them back they cannot respond to you via direct message.

It is essential that you fill out your Twitter bio. As people search and look for new people to follow, many look only at your bio, in addition to your latest tweets. Make sure your bio says something interesting enough that will make someone want to follow you. Let them know exactly what kind of expertise you provide or information you will be tweeting and provide a link to your blog or website.

Hashtags are not only useful for listening in and searching as we discussed in Chapter 2, they are also a great way to get more eyeballs on your tweets. You aren't the only one streaming tweets that include a particular hashtag. Contribute something interesting to a hashtag stream and you are likely to gain a few more followers.

Finally, when you are seeking other Twitter users, for the purpose of hoping they will follow you back, try reaching out to those individuals who follow more people then they have following them. These people are more likely to follow you back. Common etiquette is appreciated on Twitter, welcome new followers with a direct message or mention them in a tweet that thanks them for following you. It's also nice to follow people back.

 ## Video

Design and construction projects are excellent subjects for video. According to a February 2011 comScore report, more than 170 million U.S. Internet users watch online videos. However, there aren't a lot of firms in the A/E industry taking full advantage of YouTube or Vimeo yet.

Start a YouTube or Vimeo channel and upload any company videos, project videos, flythrough animations or media interviews about your company. Having all of these videos uploaded to a specific company channel on YouTube not only presents an organized video portfolio, but helps each video promote each other. For example, as a potential customer finds one of your videos, your other videos are likely to show up in the right hand bar. As you upload your videos, be sure to write a detailed description for each one, keeping your keyword phrases in mind. Google owns YouTube and often displays videos in addition to text search listings, so this is another opportunity to make your listing stand out.

Keep videos short. Thirty to 60 second videos are ideal for most watchers. You may think you need a longer run depending on your specific goals, but in most cases, anything more than five minutes is really too long. With a YouTube account, you are able to not only track how many views your video is getting but see exactly the point in your video where a viewer stopped watching. This will give you a good indication of how long is too long and which pieces of your video are not interesting.

 **Blogging**

Blogging provides an excellent opportunity to develop more thoughtful opinions and to share insightful information, as it naturally allows more space than a short tweet, comment or post. For most folks in the A/E industry, the content they post on their blog is the core information that they then promote throughout other social tools. For instance, a company may post a blog entry with an article about a new project. After the blog is posted, they can use Twitter and Facebook to post a link to the blog and provide a snippet of what the entry is about.

Unless your blog is meant for internal eyes only, don't use an internal company blog system or custom built blog software for your blog. If you do, you are not taking advantage of all the social aspects and networking opportunities available. Having a blog on a blog network, such as WordPress, Tumblr or Blogger, opens you up to an entire network of related blogs. Plus it makes life a whole lot easier, as you have access to the latest promotional tools.

Simply go to wordpress.com or blogger.com and sign up for a free blog. You'll be ready to post your first article in 20 minutes. Blogs not only give you an easy way to update your customers on new projects and company news, they also present the opportunity to gain free search traffic. Blogs help search engines find your site because blogs are largely text based (which search engines love). When you've titled your blog, categories, articles and posts using your keywords they naturally lend themselves to link building (giving easy ways for people to share content). Plus, your blog will be a part of the WordPress or Blogger network, which also helps build link popularity and exposure as the title of your blog will automatically appear on other blogs related to your topic.

Although you can use a blog for updating product and service information, think about using it to build relationships and expand your brand. Express opinions, and seek comments and feedback. Here are a few other ways to promote your blog:

>> Seek similar blogs (that don't compete with your business) and post comments when you have something to add andwhen it's relevant include a link back to your blog. The key to doing this right is to post something of value. If it sounds like spam or seems as if you are just trying to get a link, the owner of the blog will likely remove your post. Always aim to add value with everything you post online. People don't have tolerance for blatant spam. In addition to posting, you can also contact the blogger directly and invite him or her to write a guest blog for your site or even exchange blog posts for a week. This opens you both up to new audiences.

>> Ask for comments. Blogs are designed to be commented on, so close your blog with a question. Encourage people to give opinions. Sometimes being a little controversial is a great way to spark comments and make your blog go viral! And once you get some responses, provide follow up posts and answers related to the commenter's question. Keep the dialogue going as long as possible.

>> Give some thought to the title of the blog post. Take time to craft an attention grabbing headline along with an interesting photo. (You can purchase stock photos for a few dollars at bigstockphoto.com or shutterstock.com). Using keywords in your headline will not only let search engines find you, but will also help your chances of showing up in the feeds of other related blogs in your network. In addition to the keywords, the headline should be written to encourage readers to click.

"For anyone just getting started with social media marketing, keep in mind that your attitude is the most important consideration," states Christine Morris with Construction Specialties. "If engaging in this type of work is a chore, you're likely not going to get much out of it. Go into it with a sense of adventure. Do your research. Watch. Listen. Join the conversation and have fun with it!"

Chapter 4
Engaging Your Most Valuable Asset

The number of corporations that actually block the use of any form of social media during work hours will amaze you. According to a 2011 openDNS study, 14% of companies block Facebook from company computers — compared to only 1% blacklisting pornography sites. However, keeping employees from engaging on social networks can prevent a company from leveraging its most powerful assets — knowledgeable, creative and passionate employees.

When you allow employees outside the marketing department to get involved in online conversations, your brand has the ability to provide real insight and valuable conversations on projects and expertise related to your business goals. These conversations naturally go beyond pushing a PR-crafted mission statement and, particularly in intellectual and technical fields like architecture, engineering, planning and environmental services, your employees can be the key to your authentic voice. These conversations help humanize your brand and build real relationships with clients, potential clients, and subconsultants in a way that direct mail or other one-way conversation channels just can't provide.

So unless your employees and partners are engaged in top-secret projects, let them talk about it! Chances are, you're working on some very innovative, creative and exciting projects that you want to promote. Allowing your employees and other stakeholders to share openly about projects and experiences they are most passionate about lends itself naturally to exciting, genuine and viral content on the social web. And everyone from project management to business development to human resources can get involved in the social space.

"It's the ideal way to highlight the people who drive our firm forward. We're more than Building Information Modeling (BIM) models and calculators; we're also the people behind the work: guide dog raisers, teachers, philanthropists and music video performers," says Michael Pinzuti, web manager at the international structural engineering firm Thornton Tomasetti[1]. "Social channels allow us to share, promote and celebrate exactly who we really are. If the firm's website represents the polished front-door view of the company, social media

---

1 http://www.thorntontomasetti.com

represents an open window allowing a richer understanding of all the dimensions of who we are and how we work."

Identifying internal social media collaborators

If you are leading your company's social media program and internal contributors aren't knocking down your door, you may need to seek out these individuals. For medium and large firms — especially those with multiple offices — communicating within the company's internal networks is essential for coordinating your external social media effort. The corporate communications department at St Louis, Missouri –based global architecture firm HOK[2] began its "Life at HOK" blog in 2008 by connecting with the firm's global HR network. They asked each office's HR department to nominate a blogger for their location. There are likely many internal communities bound by some common interest or shared goal within your firm. However, finding the less obvious networks can present a challenge unless your firm uses some type of technology to support these networks.

For London, England-based engineering design firm Arup[3], the internal social network is part of the firm's culture. "Arup's 9,000–10,000 staff moves like a smaller firm — I think it's because of our internal networks," states Arup Senior Foresight and Sustainability Consultant Francesca Birks. "People care about quality of work. Sharing information and experience, and coordinating between regions and cities, helps each other be more effective. They establish

---

2   http://www.hoklife.com
3   http://www.arup.com

a familiarity with people in other parts of the world because they've been sharing over these networks."

Providence, Rhode Island-based interior architecture firm DiLeonardo International[4] describes its work environment as collaborative with "no bureaucracy or departments," and uses social media tools to help employees (located across five offices in five countries and multiple time zones) do their jobs. According to Eric Zuena, the firm's director of operations, "We are not the prototype organization where each of our offices are working on separate projects in separate silos. We're all working together in different time zones on the same projects. We're sharing work and communicating with staff across the world daily."

Multi-directional communications tools, such as Microsoft SharePoint or an internal blog, support employee collaboration and information sharing. These internal tools borrow from social media to help build internal networks and to foster idea sharing and collaboration. Facebook-like functions allow employees to personalize their profiles and update their colleagues on their projects and perspectives. Internal, Twitter-like micro-blogging tools let employees query the whole firm and get real-time responses from colleagues with relevant knowledge and experience. As more people within the firm use these tools as a part of their daily work, they become invaluable as a resource for tapping into the firm's total mindshare so that employees can apply the knowledge to any project. And by creating a democratic space internally, not only can employees post messages and queries to coworkers and interact with those who

---

4 http://www.dileonardo.com

comment, but they can also initiate conversations and ask questions too.

Buying and installing the new software system is the easy part. In DiLeonardo's case, they are using software called Synthesis from Knowledge Architecture that connects to commonly used back-end systems for A/E firms (i.e., Deltek Vision, Newforma Project Center, and Axomic OpenAsset) to make it easier for anyone to search for information. The social part of the tool creates a forum for employees to share knowledge and make the most of their colleagues' expertise. Read DiLeonardo's testimonial sidebar for insights on how the firm got its employees to use the tools that now support its communal work environment.

DiLeonardo's Case Study
Social Intranet

For most medium and large firms, inter-office communications becomes a huge hurdle. The next generation of internal communications, beyond intranets, has arrived. The growth of social media has spawned some intriguing internal tools that let companies and their employees communicate multi-directionally. This conversational version of the Intranet can help create new connections and share knowledge across offices and departments — if staff and leadership are willing to embrace the tools.

Since not everyone is immediately comfortable sharing and connecting with colleagues in this way, firms need to spark a shift in the way employees communicate and accomplish their work in order to benefit from these new tools. DiLeonardo, an interiors architecture firm based in Providence, Rhode Island, describes their ongoing efforts to make their firm more social.

Testimonial: Interview with Eric Zuena, director of operations for Providence, R.I.-based DiLeonardo.

Challenge: Our biggest struggle is to unify our global staff. We're all working together in different time zones on the same projects. We're sharing work and communicating with staff across the world daily. Without a relationship, without a face to the name and without an easy way to encourage communication, there is a lack of accountability or commitment and, for some, even a lack of ownership and job satisfaction.

If someone is not interested in new design trends, someone's birthday or anniversary, whether our last presentation was successful or any of the piles of other data that SharePoint (a Microsoft web application) houses for us, one could perform his or her daily duties without visiting the site at all. We found ourselves asking, "How could we best put this particular investment to work?"

Strategy: Make it impossible for employees to not use it.

Without an overlay of a third party software to integrate specific project related files (CAD, BIM, PSDs, etc), there is a certain level of "force feeding" that takes place. We started with a team of four to six people and debated which documents, workflows or templates we could move from our network drives to our SharePoint framework that would force people to go there. We considered the most intuitive locations for each. Then, we moved the data to SharePoint and waited for the obvious questions to surface, "where did the PO form go...who deleted ADA standards...what happened to our restaurant menus?" We were able to answer all these questions with the same simple answer.

Make regular and relevant updates to content:
To manage the content, every subsite (or tab) of our SharePoint framework has what we call a chief editor. Each of the chief editors is responsible for a small team of two to three people that listen and gather ideas and suggestions from our global staff. That team is also responsible for keeping their subsite active with blogs and other current information. If the team decides that they'd like to improve, remove or rebuild a feature in their framework, they work with our internal IT department to make the change. The change is then assessed and analyzed to ensure that the time it takes to make the improvement will be justified by the growth or efficiency it creates. If it is a bigger change, we would refer back to Knowledge Architecture (knowledge architecture and information systems consultancy) to assist with the custom feature.

Different disciplines find value in different features:

>> Business development — the ability to mine data from past

projects to customize and showcase the most appropriate projects to acquire new work.

>> Younger designers — links to popular resources and products.

>> Project managers — dashboard to all our reference and code material.

>> Administrators — workflows we've integrated with Infopath [Microsoft software that streamlines form downloads and submittals] for daily tasks like requests for time off, transmittals, meeting minutes.

Lesson: The consistency of our dedicated users fluctuates. While we all have the best intentions to participate/ contribute/share, there are days it just doesn't happen. If we were able to take the next logical step of integrating an overlay of Organice or Newforma, [tools that integrate industry specific files like CAD and BIM] this inconsistency would be resolved.

Results: We used to have the most trouble keeping our colleagues informed of some of the most simplistic data like, alerting staff of an individual's travel, successful presentations, office holidays, etc. And some information such as educating designers about a furniture manufacturer in Shenzhen, China or a donation that an office made to a charity would never make it around the firm.

The social end of our SharePoint framework provides

information that we'd normally have to dig up in Deltek [A/E industry accounting software] or wait for our annual office party group photo to finally arrive to learn who's who in each office. Now, employees who don't have the luxury of building in-person relationships with people in other offices still have a sense of each other.

To quote Henry Ford, "Coming together is a beginning, staying together is progress, and working together is success." Ultimately, success depends on the initial problems you originally determine to resolve. For us, improving our collaboration was paramount.

Resources:

www.dileonardo.com   sharepoint.microsoft.com

www.knowledge-architecture.com   www.cadac.com/organice

www.newforma.com   www.deltek.com

Free blogging sites like WordPress make it easy to create a private blog for "internal eyes" only, without having to depend on IT. WordPress, by default, is meant to be a public forum. However, you can also use it internally by opting to protect your posts with a password or keep them completely private. As shown in figure 4.1, simply click on the edit link next to "Visibility: Public" under the "Publish" options, to select the desired visibility for your posts.

Aside from supporting the basic communications needs of the company, these tools can be a gold mine for someone tasked with leading social media for the firm. Tap into these tools (as a contributor and as a listener) because they can provide a spring of ideas, knowledge and possible resources for your external social media efforts. The culture of social media is about engaging and sharing. It makes perfect sense to start with your own community of employees. By leveraging internal communications tools to grow your network of resources and ideas, the external social media program you create can make the most of the ambitious and authentic personalities within.

A good way to get a sense for who is inclined to serve as your external social media accomplices is to find out who is already personally using Facebook, LinkedIn, Twitter, etc. Some internal communications tools have a survey function built in. If yours doesn't, applications like SurveyMonkey make it really easy (and free if you keep it short) to survey and monitor results quickly. This information can provide a valuable benchmark for future surveys or base data to track your social media progress.

Share your findings internally as part of a campaign to keep social media in the front of employees' minds. Reach employees who haven't adopted the internal tools yet by using other internal vehicles, such as printed posters hung in common areas or an email blast. Make sure each communication about your social media program invites them to participate in the "behind the scenes" efforts that go into creating the external content.

Ask staff to like, follow, subscribe to or join the company pages and accounts — and ask them to refer their industry friends and contacts to the accounts as well. Make your external social media objectives clear and include information on how they can participate.

for internal eyes only

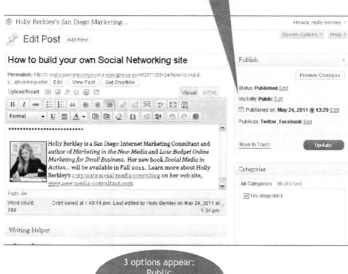

Click "edit" next to Visibility before your post your blog to see options.

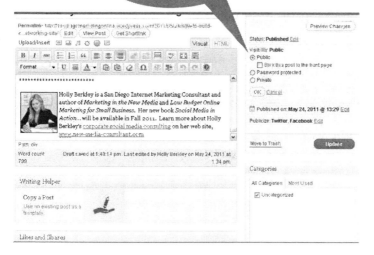

3 options appear:
Public
Password Protected
Private

As you populate your external blog and other networks with new content, use your internal tools to encourage employees to comment and share by posting hyperlinked blog headlines. Share external social media accomplishments with the group. Pass along compliments to your contributors through these visible internal channels. For example: "Jane Doe's opinion blog post was picked up by three widely read blogs, drew six thoughtful comments and we saw a 66% spike in blog traffic." Bringing these accomplishments to your employees' attention helps validate your social media efforts through quantifiable results.

Internal communications tools are also great resources for sharing your upcoming external social media plans. Let staff know what topics you are researching for future external blog posts through an editorial calendar that sets some preliminary dates for when you'll blog on a particular topic and allow staff to submit projects or ideas to you in advance. Ask your readers specific questions to help you develop these topics, i.e., "Does anyone know a source for this type of research?" or "Have we used this technology on any of our projects?"

Keep your eyes and ears open for internal mentions of material that can be re-purposed. These materials might include presentations given at events or conferences, articles or white papers that an employee has written, general research that was conducted for a project or even popular internal conversation threads. With a little work, you can break down these materials into singular ideas and reuse them as blog posts. If there is a strong visual or video component, create a slideshow or a video summary and make available on the firm's YouTube channel, and then promote them through Twitter, Facebook, or LinkedIn.

In most firms, subgroups around a particular interest that may cross departments and offices, like sustainability, are popular activity centers. Collectively, these can serve as a wealth of information, ideas and sources. Take stock of the people who are most comfortable engaging internally and the topics they gravitate toward. These employees can include subject-matter experts with knowledge to share or simply people who are comfortable giving feedback and extending conversations in social forums. Contact these people individually to consider ways they can help outside the firewall as well. Encourage them to contribute a blog post, submit a comment, man the Twitter account or even just to forward interesting data and articles that are worthy of tweeting or posting.

Connect with the undercurrent of ego that is common in the design professions by aiming the spotlight on individuals or their work. This tactic can pay off in their loyalty and interest in helping you the next time around. Not everyone will make time for social media, so focus on demonstrating success for those who will. You are likely to stir up a healthy competition among colleagues and possibly find new contributors.

You can also create your own subgroup or internal community to help keep the people who contribute to your external social media program informed of what is going on. HOK uses an internal help blog to house troubleshooting tips and suggestions to bring newly added blog-team members up to speed. To keep the blog front of mind with bloggers, the corporate communications team sends them a bi-weekly blog update that includes kudos, blog traffic reports and content suggestions.

Involving the whole organization

For many firms, social media is driven by the marketing or communications staff even if they may not be the primary voices heard on these channels. Even in cases where marketing and communications are not leading the firm's efforts, they should play a vital role in social media. In fact, no one in your company should get unleashed on the social web without a strategic plan, crafted in sync with your firm's goals and its marketing and communications groups. Just as corporations have brand guidelines that establish logos, colors and tone of voice, so should you spend time to craft social media guidelines that any employee who engages on the social web should adhere to.

Companies like Zappos boast more than 500 employees using personal Twitter accounts to help promote the company's ideals and products. Best Buy bravely empowers more than 150,000 of their employees to join customer conversations throughout the social web. And we are now seeing more A/E companies follow suit. In fact, after HMC Architects launched its external blog and became more active in Facebook and Twitter in the spring of 2010, they quickly realized the importance of having a well-crafted social media policy in place so that employees could participate.

"By opening access to social media, HMC is exploring how online conversations can empower our employees to share their expertise with clients, industry peers, and the communities in which we operate," wrote the firm's Public Relations Manager Nick Bryan in an internal memo. "Participation in social media allows us all to participate in a larger conversation related to the work we are doing at HMC and the issues and values we care about."

Bryan went on to explain that the firm must balance the benefits of empowering employees to chat online on the company's behalf against any negative consequences. After all, anything posted, commented on or tweeted is public and forever online. Therefore, guidelines must be put in place before allowing any employee, whether it's one or 150,000, to participate on behalf of the firm on the social web.

Employee training

Take time to train your staff on social media best practices as well as what they are encouraged to talk about versus what information should remain private. This training could range from the distribution of an official policy and a list of dos and don'ts to formal training sessions as official and comprehensive as any other type of in-house training. You may even consider hiring an outside social media training consultant to help you develop and set up guidelines to best fit your company's values, goals and mission. After all, how your employees talk about your company will be in the public eye.

Nokia, the mobile phone manufacturer, requires employees to complete a six-part social media certification before they can become active on the social web. Best Buy is able to successfully manage its

150,000 customer service and tech reps who use social media by conducting ongoing training and conferences.

One of the earliest A/E industry entrants to social media, architecture firm HOK, has 1,800 employees worldwide and 48 active contributors to its "Life at HOK" blog. According to the firm's Social Media Leader and Senior Writer John Gilmore, "developing a strong foundation and training was an essential element to making the Life at HOK blog successful." In 2008, when the firm initiated the "HOK Network," HOK corporate communications wrote a Blogger Manifesto that outlined the creative vision and goals for the blog. They also wrote a HOK blog policy to cover topics like etiquette and confidentiality. "Although bloggers always decide what to post, they commit themselves to client confidentiality, professionalism, mutual respect and good taste," Gilmore says.

The HOK corporate communications team also hosted a two-day, in-person training session in St. Louis, Mossouri. for employee bloggers to learn about the concept, receive training on how to use the software and to get to know each other. Gilmore says that the firm rarely edits or manages the bloggers. "We do send gentle reminders to infrequent bloggers asking whether they want to remain as active bloggers or move to 'inactive' status. And occasionally, we contact bloggers to suggest posts that are relevant to their expertise or current events."

As you look to develop your own guidelines, here are our top five recommended rules that will benefit your company:

A list of best practices

Develop a list of social media best practices. Take pieces from the list we have created at the end of this chapter and add a few that may be central to your firm's brand and mission. Make sure all employees who post anything to the Internet on behalf of your company are aware of and understand the list. A well-thought-out list of best practices is crucial to avoiding a potential PR or legal nightmare that can occur as a result of an employee posting an inappropriate comment online.

Separate personal and professional accounts

Ask employees to create separate accounts for work-related interactions. This separation helps reduce confusion when employees start using their social profiles to post personal information, such as pictures of their family vacations. In Facebook, for example, you can have one company page, and then make key employees an "Admin." This way they can post information directly to your company Facebook page outside of their personal Facebook profile. However, keep in mind that depending on privacy settings customers can still click on an Admin's picture to see employee personal profile pictures, bio, and names of groups that employee belongs to. (The employee's Facebook posts stay private unless the employee "friends" that customer.) This overlap of personal and professional profiles is one example of why employees should follow the best practices lists. Let employees know that even items posted on personal blogs and profiles reflects their professionalism as a whole. Remind employees that everything gets connected in some way and comes back to the individual's perceived professionalism.

Ongoing training and open discussion

Social media continues to grow and expand with new rules, widgets, tools and sites popping up almost daily. Set up periodic meetings with your contributing staff to talk about new trends as well as let employees share their ideas about what's working and what isn't. When appropriate, adjust your guidelines accordingly. Social media is a constantly changing medium and your guidelines should stay flexible.

Make it easy for employees to engage in a consistent way

Take a tip from Best Buy's social media tool kit and have your marketing team help employees with profile pictures and provide them with company logos and approved imagery so that anyone posting on your behalf projects a consistent look.

Define your goals for employee engagement in social media

Part of your employee training should include defining an agenda for why you are allowing them to participate on the social web in the first place. Is it to share knowledge and expertise? Demonstrate values and leadership in your field? Gain real feedback to improve existing projects? Build relationships in hopes of attaining more future business? HOK began its social media presence with the goal of changing the perception of the firm from "HOK, the big company" to "HOK, the creative people" and the firm pursued this goal by shining light on the people and personalities behind their projects and on HOK's creative culture. HOK's social arsenal now consists of seven blogs, two Twitter handles, Facebook, LinkedIn,Flickr, a YouTube channel, Scribd.com for publications, Slideshare.net for presentations, Visualcv.com for multimedia resume submittals and Delicious.com for social bookmarking. For

HOK BIM Solutions Blog

Firm: HOK, St. Louis, Missouri

Project: HOK BIM Solutions Blog

Challenge: Very early on, HOK has been a proponent of object-based collaboration (the precursor to BIM). In 1995, the firm was a founding member of the International Alliance for Interoperability), which was later re-branded as BuildingSMART. By the late 1990s, HOK was adopting BIM using Autodesk's Architectural Desktop and then in 2002 shifted to Autodesk's Revit. As a demonstration of their commitment to interoperability, the firm published their CAD standards for anyone to download. In a press release from April 2007, HOK announced that it would apply BIM to all of its new projects. CEO Patrick MacLeamy explained, "We're doing this quite openly so that others can see what we do and emulate it." The internal BIM group, known as HOK buildingSMART BIM community, was tasked with supporting this effort.

Objective: Share HOK's BIM lessons learned to cut down the redundancy of finding answers to the BIM issues that users come across in their daily work.

Strategy: On July 21, 2007, then HOK Vice President and Firmwide BIM Manager Miles Walker, along with then Senior Vice President and Firmwide Director of BIM Mario Guttman, launched the HOK CAD Solutions blog to create a running list of the issues and answers as a resource for HOK users and external CAD users. The blog tended to talk about BIM as one aspect of

CAD. Unfortunately the common usage made CAD equivalent to AutoCAD, so HOK changed the blog's name to HOK BIM Solutions Blog. Even with the new, more specific name, the blog was always intended to be broader than just Revit and a few, but not many, postings discussed 3dsMax, SketchUp and other tools.

Blog content was contributed by the HOK buildingSMART BIM community, which consisted of the five members of the firmwide BIM team and the one or two BIM staff in each of the offices. The group had regular conference calls and met in person approximately every other year, but they primarily communicated through an internal email list called HOK BIM support. "Anyone could pose issues there. We had some protocols for how the subsequent replies were managed, like 'don't Reply All please.' These threads, which often included screen shots and other images, sometimes became the basis for a blog post," recalled Guttman. "We also called each other and used WebEx a lot [to have video teleconferences]." Ultimately, it was the responsibility of the person who initially posed a question to the broader group, to connect with all the people offering advice, determine the solution and contribute the findings to the group in the form of a blog post.

Guttman and Walker established some basic ground rules for the blog:

Include
>> Solutions to problems that are likely to occur generally.
>> Interesting work processes that are of general interest.

Exclude

>> General commentary about the industry.

>> Personal opinions on the direction of HOK or the industry

>> Problems without complete solutions.

>> Solutions or processes that would only apply in a limited context.

Etiquette

>> Be constructive, polite and positive.

Results: The HOK BIM Solutions blog includes the right level of content for its intended audience — technically sophisticated and relevant to the readers' actual work. It also presents this content well — it's clearly organized and there are lots of graphics to help explain the text.

Even though there isn't a huge amount of public engagement, the internal audience was always intended to be the primary reader. The public does read it, though and their occasional contributions are significant — not just "me too" posts. In fact, one outside contributor, David Light, was the author of a similar well-read blog (http://autodesk-revit.blogspot.com) and was ultimately recruited to join HOK. Light is now an associate and Revit specialist at HOK's London office and is currently one of the managers for the HOK BIM Solutions blog. He also continues to maintain his personal blog, which HOK now includes in their list of HOK Network links.

One could also conclude that the blog has supported the firm's position as being ahead of the industry curve in its use of technology. BIM has been the subject, or critical to the subject, of more than 20 articles about HOK since the blog launched.

Ultimately, the blog has been successful because it is a useful resource for the people for which it was written, the internal HOK buildingSMART BIM Community and BIM users outside the firm.

Lessons

The social media culture is a sharing one. For firms that have deep expertise and the boldness to give away their lessons learned, social media is a natural fit. HOK's BIM Solutions Blog is a good example of the extended value of the skills and know-how of employees. Showcasing and giving away this knowledge is more than a benevolent contribution to the development of younger architects and firms, it is a display of the firm's confidence in its expertise. Blogs require a steady flow of new content and a sustained investment in talent and time. When done right, this approach can attract the type of professionals who want to work with — and learn from — top notch colleagues and make for a fantastic showpiece for a client who wants to know that he or she is hiring the best.

Give it away and it returns

"One of the challenges of keeping blogs updated is exactly that, keeping the blogs updated and getting people to contribute well written articles that do not need rewording and recomposing into a blog format," shared Walker, who is now the corporate BIM coordinator for KEO Design in Kuwait. Both of the blog originators are now at other firms, and in the past few months the posts are less frequent. Walker offers this analogy, "I like to think of it as taking on responsibilities of owning a puppy. For a while it seems exciting new, fun and good to play with (like Twitter, blogs and Facebook). Then the dog grows and the fun becomes less and more of a chore as routine sets in and the dog matures, but he still needs to be fed and watered!"

Blogs require constant care and feeding, don't adopt one without understanding this responsibility.

Resources:

www.hok.com

http://hokbimsolutions.blogspot.com/

http://autodesk-revit.blogspot.com

the story behind the firm's first social media venture, read the case study sidebar on how the firm launched the HOK BIM Solutions Blog to support the industry's adoption of CAD and later BIM.

Once you define these goals for social media, realize that not all employees will (or should) engage on social networks in the same way. Take inventory of the strengths and weaknesses of certain individuals to determine the best way they can use their time on the social web. For some employees, the most valuable thing they can do will be to listen. By setting up Google Alerts with keywords around the projects they are working on, they can gather real-time information and conversations as they happen online and then report back to their group. Employees can also play a role at amplifying positive conversations that may help move along projects or increase company influence. After they discover and identify specific conversations, encourage them to retweet or comment on posts to give extend its reach and shelf life on the social web.

Choosing the right employees to carry the company voice

When we were asked to set up a social media strategy for Lake Flato[5], a San Antonio, Texas-based architecture firm, the first thing we did after sitting down with the principals to define the objectives and overall goals of the social media initiative was to interview their staff. We asked a range of employees, from the marketing coordinator to a graphic artist to IT to architects, questions about their existing social media use and interest. We also asked about their unique backgrounds, both professionally and personally, as well as about groups and affiliations they belonged to and were actively involved in.

Our goal was to identify employees with a genuine interest in communicating on behalf of the company via social networks, as well as those who could provide a fresh, thoughtful perspective that was still in alignment with the company's overall mission, brand and goals. Plus, it helps to identify employees who already have genuine ties to existing social networks, affiliations or groups that can mesh well with the overall goals of the campaign to help propel a new social media effort more quickly.

Advising on the right employees to help carry the voice of Lake Flato in its new social media program got easier when we learned that the company had already set up an internal community with SharePoint that was run by staff. They proudly called this internal social network

5 http://www.lakeflato.com

FlakeNet. Here the staff posted awards, upcoming industry events as well as "lessons learned" and important documents needed for client projects. Originally created to be a learning and work resource, FlakeNet evolved into a place to post personal announcements about office sporting events, birthdays and engagements. The staff even posted humorous pictures, such as staff celebrity look-a-likes and "guess whose baby picture this is?" snapshots. In the process, the staff was able to find a common way to bond and get to know each other. The fact that this information was not for the public eye gave employees more freedom to express themselves and their opinions and essentially form their voice within the company. Choosing the right voices to carry the Lake Flato message to the public became easier after observing how staff engaged on their internal social network. These observations helped pave the strategy and structure for the external social networking plan and helped us to set realistic expectations for how the FlakeNet activity could carry over to a more public forum. For many companies, setting up an internal social network can serve as an ideal testing and training ground before launching a public campaign.

Recommended employee guidelines

Employee guidelines are not widespread yet in the A/E industry, therefore the best employee guidelines come from other industries (with many posted online for public view). Top companies like Best Buy, Dell, Zappos, and Nokia along with a few A/E firms like HOK, Arup, HMC Architects and Thornton Tomasetti offer insight for a list of important social media guidelines and best practices your firm should implement before allowing employees to use the social web on your behalf.

1. Only engage if you can have a constructive conversation.

In other words, not all posts related to your project or industry need a comment. Recognize the difference between an angry community member's rant about your designs for an upcoming development and a concerned resident that just needs to understand the project better.

2. Engage only when you can make an impact.

Strive to add value with each engagement. "Engaging in online conversations is a tremendous opportunity for highlighting the thought leadership activities taking place at the firm," writes Nick Bryan in HMC Architects' Social Media Policy. "Be sure that what you're posting adds value to the practice of architecture and is promoting the firm's values."

Always adding value includes sticking to your area of expertise. Employees should only comment if it falls within an area for which they specifically work first hand.

3. Be transparent. Be smart. Be respectful. Be professional. Be human. But also be yourself.

These are key traits that appear on social media policies as important characteristics for engaging in social media. All posts should always maintain a positive tone and stay respectful of others — especially competitors.

More and more, employees will have their own blog or website outside of what they are doing for their company. HMC Architects addresses this issue in its social media policy with the following statement:

"Ultimately what you post is your responsibility, so be sure it reflects you positively. Please make it clear to your readers that the views you express are yours alone and that they do not necessarily reflect the views of HMC, our clients, or your coworkers. To help reduce the potential for confusion, we would suggest the following notice — or something similar — in a reasonably prominent place on your site (e.g., at the bottom of your "about me" page):

The views expressed on this site are mine alone and do not necessarily reflect the views of my employer.

Many bloggers put a disclaimer on their front page saying who they work for, but that they're not speaking officially. This is good practice, but may not have much legal effect. It's not necessary to post this notice on every page, but please use reasonable efforts to draw attention to it — if at all possible, from the home page of your site."

4. Identify what information should never be made public.

Work with your legal team and speak with your clients to understand what issues employees cannot discuss. In the Thornton Tomasetti "Social Media Dos and Don'ts," the firm encourages employees to "understand what can and cannot be talked about. Things said in passing in the hallways at [Thornton Tomasetti] are not necessarily open for conversation outside the firm. When in doubt, treat it like the nuclear football. A good test: Will this information help us help our clients?"

In general, it's important to ask staff to think before they post and to run any information that may be sensitive by a designated marketing or communications leader before publication. Along the same lines, make sure imagery employees post is approved.

5. Designate times when employees can use the social web during work hours.

Some best practices lists state: "Don't let social media activity interfere with your work." It's a good idea to set designated times when you allow employees to visit these sites. Many companies that allow employees to engage on social media only do so outside of normal business hours. Our advice? It really depends on your overall goals, and many times, you want to comment when conversations happen. Sometimes, waiting until "after business hours" is too late. Be sure to have Google Alerts or other social media tools in place that at least one key individual is in charge of monitoring and who can alert the right internal people when they need to provide comments. As you read Chapter 7, about measuring and tracking your social media program's effectiveness, you will be able to understand if there is a preferred time of day when employees should participate in social media efforts.

Chapter 5
Expert Positioning

As a professional service firm, your company's reputation relies on the knowledge and success of the individuals you employ. In fact, this is the primary reason we encourage clients to make their people the focus of their social media marketing program, instead of the firm brand. This is not a new strategy. According to our research, 88% of survey respondents are using social media specifically to position their experts.

The importance of leveraging an individual's reputation in a professional services firm became clear to us during the research and writing of this book. In one case, a client happened to be seated next to us on a cross-country flight just days after a well-known A/E firm had announced that it was acquired by a larger firm. The client admitted, "I don't care if the firm is owned by someone else. I don't care what the name on the sign is. I will continue to do work with the firm as long as the principal I trust is there. If he moves on or retires before I am able to get to know and trust someone else, I will go somewhere else to work with a person I know I can depend on."

Through your projects and daily work, you build trust and expertise with your clients in the same way other professional services firms such as law firms and accounting firms operate. Social media provides a way to enhance those personal relationships and keep client bonds thriving long after a project is complete. Keeping the relationships alive via social media helps establish long term trust which in turn opens your firm up to future projects with that client, and ideally, will open your firm up to that client's trusted social network as well.

In the past, industry thought leaders were established through numerous speaking engagements, published works and featured interviews in industry publications. Today, thanks to the social web, you can start building your reputation as a thought leader right now.

Being an expert in one's field goes beyond simply sharing links to articles others have written, posting your latest projects to Facebook or joining the latest LinkedIn group. These social media tactics are great for marketing your firm and keeping it in the forefront of your client's eyes, but do not necessarily qualify you as an industry expert or thought leader.

Online experts are motivated by a genuine curiosity in their field and continue to ask questions, develop new ideas and share knowledge that in turn helps them develop a loyal following and promote the research in that particular field of study. In social media, loyal followers share your ideas with their social groups. The more exposure you get for industry contributions, the faster you can become a recognized expert.

According to Francesca Birks, Arup's senior foresight[1] and sustainability consultant in New York, New York, those who find the most success in establishing themselves as thought leaders are those who are most comfortable in leadership roles. "These people want to spar intellectually. These are people who see the big picture [and understand] that there is more going on beyond the day to day of winning work and pleasing clients," explains Birks. These individuals have the confidence to develop and support innovative ideas, while displaying the ambition to be a part of shaping the future of the company.

Investing in multiple thought leadership roles within your company

In the past, thought leadership roles were left to the CEO and company founders. Today's social media channels make room for many levels of expert voices including employees with unique or

---

1 www.foresight.com

specific skill sets and knowledge bases. These potential "subject matter experts" are employees who thrive when given the opportunity to share ideas and crave a fresh stream of innovative thoughts and conversations for a fulfilling professional life. Firms that give these employees the possibility and support of the firm's resources to become subject matter experts are betting on the potential of these individuals –as change agents and as leaders. The bet is that the time and effort used by this person will pay off in firm and personal thought leadership potency.

For some firm leaders, the concern of publicizing an employee via social media over someone who has ownership in the company is perilous. The thought of investing money and brand equity in a non-ownership employee only to have him or her walk or be lured away by the competition is too risky.

However, Chris Parsons, founder of Knowledge Architecture[2] in San Francisco, California, is an advocate for more people taking on the role of thought leaders in the A/E industry. He notes that "Thought leadership is a team sport. It's about asking questions and posing ideas." Social media is a fantastic forum for this.

Birks also advocates reaching out to others to build a solid thought leadership campaign. "There is no way 11 people can be responsible for all thought leadership for our company," she says. In order to cover more of the social web and keep conversations relevant, Birks' company encourages colleagues and friends to help share ideas, ask questions and participate in their thought leadership campaigns.

---

2   www.knowledge-architecture.com

Become part of the conversation

Just as social media can be a powerful tool for amplifying your communications efforts; it is an equally powerful listening tool. By joining a LinkedIn group and following specific Twitter hashtags (as mentioned earlier in this book), you can keep up-to-date on new projects and concerns of your colleagues. Google Alerts is another easy way to get notified anytime the media or other websites are discussing a subject that makes sense for you to weigh in on. You can take this idea of social media listening even further by using a professional social media listening or monitoring tool. Just type in "social media listening" or "social media monitoring tools" to a search engine and you will see plenty of options. Or, for bigger companies hoping to cover more ground, use a more advanced listening and monitoring tool like Radian6. Such tools will allow you to discover your industry's hottest topics and most pressing problems and concerns. The tool works with keyword phrases and will provide you with direct links to conversations that contain those phrases. Then, once you have knowledge to contribute to these conversations, you can weigh in as an expert on those threads and start building your thought leadership credibility.

The goal, Birks explains, is that in order to be a leader, you have to be a part of the conversation. And if you aren't the best person to answer a question posed online, pull in your employee or other team member who specializes in that area. "We've looped some team member's personal blogs into the framework," says Birks. "You have to be part of a conversation if you want to be a leader in it. The alternative is that other people will crowd the space and fill the void."

Steve Mouzon of Mouzon Design[3], founder of the New Urban Guild[4] in Miami Beach, Florida,has been a promoter of the tenets of New Urbanism and practical sustainability for years. He also has a strong grasp on the role of a thought leader. Mouzon has created and nurtured his network and tapped into their common interests by sharing his ideas and useful information through workshops and networking groups. Social media came along and made all of this easier for Mouzon.

In one of Mouzon's blogs, "Useful Stuff"[5] he writes, "Social media is working magic that was unimaginable a decade ago. Once, we read the daily newspaper, watched the evening news, and followed the American Top 40. But over the past decade, we've learned how to speak to [each other] again." He continues, "Commenters on my blog posts regularly have great ideas that improve the ideas I was blogging about. This is an enormous time-saver, because I can't possibly bring all their experience to bear on the question... because I don't have their experience."

In our interview with Mouzon, he advises that anyone hoping to position themself as a thought leader become a part of a cause and promote a set of ideals, as opposed to promoting their own products or personal agenda. He explains that great ideas need networks in order for them to spread. "For example, in the past we'd share ideas by hosting a workshop with about 100-150 attendees," Mouzon explained when asked how he communicated ideas before social media. "But today, social media allows us to engage a larger group. The Facebook cause* page for the Original Green has more than 1,000 members."

3   www.mouzon.com
4   www.newurbanguild.com
5   http://usefulstuff.posterous.com/new-media-for-design-types

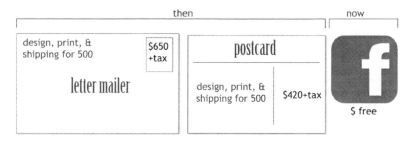

communications cost comparison of traditional versus social tactics

Bestselling author and marketing expert Seth Godin refers to these networks as tribes. In his book "Tribes: We Need You to Lead Us" (2008), Godin defines a tribe as "a group of people connected to one another, connected to a leader, and connected to an idea. For millions of years, human beings have been part of one tribe or another. A group needs only two things to be a tribe: a shared interest and a way to communicate." He goes on to explain, "Tribes need leadership. Sometimes one person leads, sometimes more. People want connection and growth and something new. They want change." Godin eloquently boils it down to this, "You can't have a tribe without a leader — and you can't be a leader without a tribe."

Contribute new information

Part of your role in leading the tribe of people interested in your topic is to help advance the understanding of it. Research is a great way to discover more about a subject. Explore topics that can address your clients' unmet needs and areas that can strengthen your own services and products. If it's useful to you, chances are others will be interested in learning about it as well. This is no longer the age of competitive secrecy. Social media is a great place to formulate your hypothesis and test it within your tribes. Because of its culture of openness and sharing your social networks can function like a continuous focus group. The feedback you get in return improves your next iteration of thinking. By allowing others to participate in it and help shape your thinking you create ambassadors who are willing to spread the word.

There are many ways to conduct research. For firms working in the built environment, you may already be conducting product, techniques or method research as a part of the work you do for your clients. If your findings aren't proprietary to your client and your firm owns the rights most likely there are many others who could benefit from the results of your research. Use your blog as a means of publishing the research findings and use your other networks to let more people know about it.

For a simple approach, you can use Facebook's "Question" tool to ask your friends and fans a question. LinkedIn also has a "Poll" function that can feed into your Twitter and Facebook accounts. These tools are designed to take your poll viral so that people who respond can pose the question to their network and the members of their network can pass it along to their connections, and so on.

The question, the poll results and any comments are stored on your page for anyone to view. You could just send the link to the results out to your network, or you could blog or tweet about your take on the findings. The results and your assessment of them are all very share-able bits of content. Your tribe is interested in what the data means to you — and more likely than not, they would be interested in chiming in with their perspective as well, so it doesn't hurt to ask what they think.

If you have more time and resources, you can create your own experiment — online or offline — and tap your social networks to drive people to participate.

Architecture firm OWP/P, which is now Canon Design[6] in Chicago, Illinois, partnered with furniture manufacturer VS Furniture[7] of Tauberbischofsheim, Germany and Toronto, Ontario-based design thinking firm Bruce Mau Design[8] to study the role of the learning environment in educating children. The resulting research became a book of 79 ideas for transforming teaching and learning, The Third Teacher[9]. Read the case study sidebar to learn how social media plays an important role in how The Third Teacher continues the flow of ideas that the book started.

---

6   www.cannondesign.com
7   www.vs-furniture.com
8   www.brucemaudesign.com
9   www.thethirdteacher.com

Third Teacher Case Study

Firm: Canon Design (formerly OWP/P), Chicago, Illinois

Project: The Third Teacher

Challenge: In a blog post from May 18, 2009, Trung Le notes, "Our intent was to deepen our understanding of the history, the institutions, the pedagogies and the policies that shape our idea of education. We believed that by participating in this enriching research process we would be contributing to the immense goal of making the world a better place through the education of our children."

Le is a principal and a leader in the K-12 group at Canon Design (OWP/P at the time), which has been designing schools and learning spaces for more than 50 years. In 2007, he began an exploration of ideas for reimagining how we design our schools. To conduct this, he teamed up with VS Furniture of Tauberbischofsheim, Germany that has designed and manufactured furniture for schools for more than 100 years and Toronto, Ontario-based design thinking firm, Bruce Mau Design, which designs books and helps organizations embrace change. The team was united by the Reggio Emilia educational philosophy started by Loris Malaguzzi and the parents of the villages around Reggio Emilia in Italy after World War II. According to this philosophy the educational environment is crucial and is included as one of the students' three teachers:

1. Adults, as in parents and teachers
2. Peers
3. The environments that surround them

The group researched ways to improve the role of the "third teacher," the physical learning environment, with field trips to schools around the world and interviews with other champions for changing existing learning environments. The collective began assembling a list of ideas that emerged from these experiences and these ideas became the core of their book The Third Teacher: 79 Ways You Can Use Design to Transform Teaching and Learning, which was published in March 2009. With 78 strong ideas, the collaborative ended their two-year research and publishing endeavor with one more, "79. Add to this list."

Objective: "Galvanize a movement to rethink teaching and learning." — Trung Le

Led by Trung Le and Canon Design, The Third Teacher trio needed to engage readers, teachers, students, scholars, designers, parents and others in creating and discovering more design ideas that both reacts to clients' needs and acts on the group's interests and curiosities. They also wanted input from these audiences to refine their thinking. Lastly, The Third Teacher group wanted to test these concepts in real environments. Ultimately, The Third Teacher is looking for ways to improve their techniques.

Strategy: Share ideas. Ask questions. Listen. Collaborate.

To take the 79 ideas to a broader audience, The Third Teacher collaborative moved beyond the book to mix online and offline strategies. Social media is the front door. It's the entry point for those who are just learning about the book and a bank for all the emerging research and ideas. In the physical world, Le and his Third Teacher team at Canon Design speak publicly. They meet with teachers and other education-oriented groups and they lead elementary school field trips. In the online social realm, they track and connect with other education reform advocates.

"Social media was the natural extension of our efforts," says Sarah Malin, Canon's Third Teacher researcher and anthropologist. The group of collaborators uses their blog to share offline experiences and ideas as fodder for posts. "This is

#79
add to this list

Social media is only part of the answer. The greatest impact comes when **social media** is combined with **physical marketing** and public relations innitiatives.

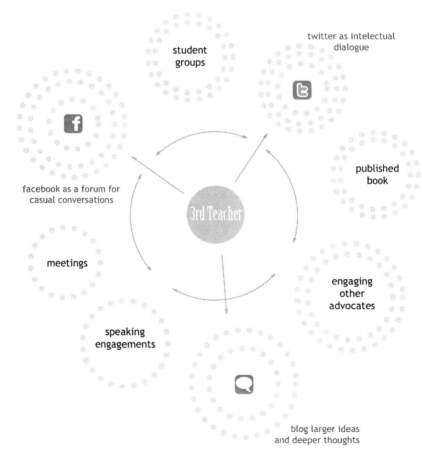

where we share the ideas that we're puzzling in our heads." Posts are shared through the Facebook page and on Twitter so that the broader audience has access to the group's latest thinking.

The group uses Twitter to listen and stay up on the big movements and change makers in education. The good examples are retweeted and passed on to their tribe through Facebook. They found that Facebook brings out more casual comments. Twitter is more practical for them and allows participation in more intellectual conversations. The Third Teacher blog is most useful for developing ideas. It's a less frequent voice but it offers deeper thoughts and the feedback tends to be more specific.

Lesson: Initially The Third Teacher group expected that the social media outlets would be a place where people would submit their well-formulated ideas, but what they received was a casual trading of thoughts. As a result, the group eventually removed the "Add an Idea" function from their blog. Malin explains, "We learned that if we want the conversation to be truly adding, these need to happen in person."

Events, like the Columbus, Ohio, Prototype Design Camp in February 2011, where Third Teacher team members participated and led a three-day immersive design workshop that asked high school juniors and seniors to change their learning experience, are more effective in discovering new ideas because idea-sharing is more interactive and the hands-on nature of the event acts as a sort of testing ground for the concepts that arise. Other events, like the TEDxReset event in Istanbul, Turkey, an independently organized event based on the Technology Entertainment Design (TED) "Ideas Worth Spreading" format where Le spoke to young people interested in "resetting" the Turkish reality, are more traditional, one-way presentations, but benefit from the video and viral format that allows The Third Teacher's ideas to be shared far beyond the walls of the auditorium. The presentation is the spark that generates higher quality feedback — both in-person following the talk and afterward via email or through one of the social networks.

Instead of abandoning social media when it didn't deliver the way they had hoped, The Third Teacher focused on what it was doing well — meeting other advocates. "We need to have a renaissance team that is multidisciplinary to bring a wealth of perspectives for stronger design," Malin explains. The new social media strategy is to bridge the online and offline worlds. "Social media is where we transition people who offer interesting comments and suggestions from followers into business collaborators." The group invites promising social media followers to in-person conferences, workshops and events. As a result they grow these relationships and connect more deeply.

Results: The Third Teacher didn't set out to position itself as a thought leader. "Trung Le has always steered us away from thinking in terms of public relations, marketing or promotion. Everything we do is to create relationships based on ideas," says Malin. As a result of following Le and his partners' curiosities they have become an authority on the emerging thinking for education design.

In addition to a steady escalation of followers and fans, a healthy level of conversation and even new collaborative working-relationships with some of the followers, these channels have brought in new business. A current client, The International School of Indiana, found them through Facebook. Social media was also how the group overheard the early plans for the education themed TEDx event in Chicago and they credit Twitter with their role in helping plan that event.

The collective effect of the entire program is also impressive. The group is bringing on one of their collaborators to enrich their team. Together they will be an architect/designer, anthropologist/designer and now an educator/designer. This additional resource will allow the program to expand its social media offerings beyond ideas. The group plans to redesign the site and create digital counterparts to the physical and analog materials (e.g. flash cards) that they use in their in-person conversations and events. Malin notes, "Technology allows our static items to evolve and adapt."

And lastly, Canon Design is launching a dedicated consulting practice for The Third Teacher that will emphasize the pre-design strategy and thinking that creates a picture of what the community needs and relates these to the designers of the physical space.

Authenticity, passion and energy are contagious.

Resources:

www.thethirdteacher.com

www.thethirdteacher.com/ourvoice

www.facebook.com/home.php#!/TheThirdTeacher

@thethirdteacher

www.vs-furniture.com

www.brucemaudesign.com

www.TED.com

www.tedxreset.com/en

We are all human. Even without intending to do so, the way you phrase a question may have a negative or positive overtone or it could lead your respondent to answer it differently than if it were phrased neutrally. Make sure you structure your undertaking in a way that is fair and doesn't produce bad science. For scientific accuracy, you need to be sure that your respondents accurately reflect the demographic you are studying. You may even consider consulting with a researcher to help you structure your study so that your results are correct.

There is a certain level of credibility associated with conducting research, so make sure your research and its results are branded with your name or your firm's name. But the real value to your reputation comes in how you interpret the results. The more effort you put into making sure your study produces good science on the front-end, the more valuable your results — and your analysis — will be. Your personal take on what the findings mean for the industry or market sector should be the subject of a communications campaign of its own.

Use as many channels (not just social media ones) as makes sense to promote your findings: press releases, email blasts, face-to-face press meetings, editorials and bylined articles, videos, speaking, workshops, social media and so on. But don't forget to position your blog at the center of this campaign and to use your tribe — in all the networks that they gather — to get the word out.

Build your fan base

Thanks to social media, Marcela Abadi Rhoads, owner of Dallas, Texas accessibility consultancy Abadi Accessibility[10], is one of only 500 registered accessibility specialists in the country. She is considered an expert in the field. Her active presence on social media sites and loyal following led to her being contacted by a publisher, which ended in a book deal. She is the author of The ADA Companion Guide, which explains the 2010 ADA standards, and is currently working on her second book. As a result of her first book and continued use of social media outreach, she is sought after by owners and architects across the country who are looking for guidance to understand the accessibility standards throughout the design and construction process.

"Social Media is a way that I became the 'expert' in my field," Rhoads explains, "The more that I post information about architecture and accessibility and the more I engage in discussions in the same area, the more exposure I get and the more credibility I receive." Rhoads' is a great example of giving away thought leadership for free and receiving it back in cash.

---

10   www.abadiaccess.com

Her approach to social media is to be an "open network and accept everyone." In other words, she always follows those who follow her on Twitter, accepts every LinkedIn connect request and accepts every Facebook friend request. "The more people I connect with the more exposure I get," she says. "It is sometimes surprising who I am connecting with. You really never know who might be a good referral source. My book would not have happened if it wasn't for my efforts with social media."

Using a blog for expert positioning

Today, it seems like everyone has a blog. In fact, according to BlogPulse.com, there were 152 million blogs on the Internet at the end of 2010. That number is expected to grow. Of course, having a blog does not automatically make you a thought leader.

In addition to posting thought-provoking, conversation-starting, innovative ideas within your industry, you need to establish a loyal following to help you extend the life of that idea, and continue to grow your audience. Even professionals who have written popular books, who participate in speaker series or have some other way to communicate ideas with large numbers of people benefit from the flexibility, reach and viral potential a blog can provide. A blog can be the most efficient way to get your ideas heard and should be the center piece of your thought leadership campaign.

Yes, a blog is an excellent place to share ideas and pose questions and get conversations started. However, even the best written blog still needs a marketing strategy behind it. And the social web lends itself perfectly to promoting blog posts. Free blog services like WordPress and Blogger come with widgets that allow you to easily connect your blog to Facebook, Twitter and other popular social news web sites to make sharing your most recent blog post easy.

Leverage existing thought leaders' blogs to promote your own ideas

A good way to start generating quality traffic to your new blog is to seek similar industry blogs that your target audience is already reading. Make sure the blog topics and their authors complement your overall goals and brand rather than compete for services. Once you've identified some good blogs that fit this description, determine which ones have the most traffic and therefore should demand more of your efforts.

Web sites such as Statsaholic.com, Compete.com and Quantcast. com allow you to type in a URL and see how much traffic that site gets. You can also see what types of audiences visit that blog by a demographic profile breakdown. Web sites like Quantcast.com even show you what other websites users visited immediately before or after that blog, which can give you additional ideas on potential websites to reach out to.

Once you've identified the top blogs that your target audience is reading, get involved in the conversation. You can post a comment with a web-link back to your blog, which should help you gain targeted traffic. However, as we mention earlier, the key to doing this right is to post something of value. If your comment or post sounds "spammy" or that you are just trying to post a link, the owner of the blog will likely remove your post. The blog owner may even block you from future posts, further defining your behavior as spam. Always aim to add true value with everything you post online. Also, people can tell when you don't take any risks in your posts; and pat answers and posts like "He said it all right there!" are quickly disregarded as disingenuous. People don't have tolerance for blatant spam. Posting anything that could be mistaken as spam or fake comments will hurt your efforts to establish yourself as a thought leader.

In addition to posting a comment on another blog, you can also contact the blogger directly and exchange blog posts for a week or schedule regular "guest posts." This opens you both up to new audiences and gives your blog more depth. Another idea is to interview the popular blogger and post an article about them on your blog. By promoting that blogger, he might promote your blog to his audience in turn.

Get conversations going on your own blog

Blogs are designed to be commented on. They are a great place to share ideas and even argue. Consider blogging on topics that are somewhat controversial, that can encourage a positive and intellectual debate. It's also a good idea to ask for comments. Let readers know that you value their input and want them to comment.

Whenever you do get a comment on your blog, make sure you respond directly and publicly to that person. It's not only polite, but it also helps keep the conversation going. Instead of simply saying "thanks for the post!" ask another question and try to keep the authentic, topic-oriented comments flowing. Another strategy to help build momentum for an important post is to go back after a few weeks and post a follow up. This helps build up link popularity and exposure for the first post. Finally, develop a thick skin. Not everyone will love all your ideas. Putting yourself out on the social web as a potential thought leader can open you up to public scrutiny. And once in a while, you will get comments that are unflattering. Fortunately, as the author of the blog, you can choose which comments are made public. You will be tempted to hide all the negative comments but in our experience in social media this can be a big mistake. If voices don't feel like they can be heard on your blog, they will stop reading. And people who are not allowed to post on your blog will likely blog to others the fact that you are running a false-blog tyranny. Let the negative posts to your blog go public even if you have to edit them a bit first. Then be confident about your ideas with your rebuttal and address that reader's negative concerns. Having a few negative comments and responding with grace and knowledge shows honesty, concern and helps build trust. You may even end up turning your nay-sayer into one of your biggest advocates.

Optimize your blog for the search engines

Search engines love blogs. Blogs are text based, which makes them very easy for search engines, such as Google and Bing, to "read" and categorize. Take a moment to use Google's free keyword research

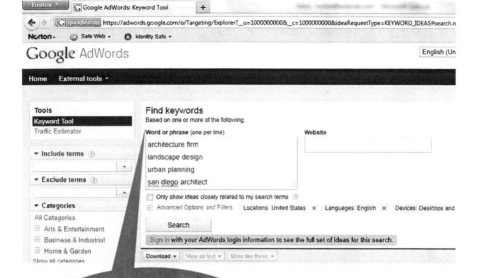

Google's free keyword tool lets you type in keywords related your firm's services, and see the global, and local average monthly searches for that term. It also lets you see how much competition a keyword phrase has.

Google will also give you a list of hundreds of other keyword phrases related to your terms that you may not have considered. The idea is to find the phrases with the highest search volume, and lowest competition.

tool. You can find it under Google Adwords[11], or search "keyword tool" on Google. As we show on the next page, you can enter keywords related to your industry and what services and ideas you hope to be found online. The keyword tool will show you a list of related terms by **1) competition** — how many other web sites are competing for that same term and **2) search volume** — how many people are actually searching for that term. You want to find the best keyword phrases that describe your business and services and that have the highest search volume and lowest competition. Once you've identified these keywords, use them whenever you can as you set up your blog. You can even use them in your blog's name, URL and in the category, also known as pages, within your blog.

When you write a new blog, you will also have the opportunity to include keywords as tags. Tags not only help search engines know more about what your blog post is about but they are also used by the blog network to categorize your post and promote it. This is important because it helps the blog network identify which other blogs may be similar to your topic and will promote your blog to that audience. For example, when you read a blog that was built with WordPress or Blogger you will often see a list of two to three links to related posts at the end of the article you just read. These links are automatically selected based on keywords used in the article's tags as well as keywords used in its headline. This is why crafting an attention-grabbing headline with keywords is so important to gaining access in front of new audiences.

---

11   google.com/sktool/

Promoting your blog post on other social networks

Most of the popular blogging platforms offer a setting to automatically post your latest entry to other social networks, such as a Twitter or Facebook account. We advise against this. Although it saves time, each of your audiences on these social networks may differ and crafting a slightly different headline and incentive to click is beneficial. Also, people you are connected to will tire quickly of receiving the exact same comment from you on multiple sites.

Use a URL shortening service like bit.ly or goo.gl to create short URL's that you can use for Twitter, LinkedIn and other social media sites. Another benefit to using these URL shorteners is that they offer the ability to track which links received the most clicks, so if you use different links for different social media sites, you can see which site your blog traffic is getting more traffic from. This provides you with added data you can use to improve your messaging. (More on tracking in Chapter 7.)

Finally, always include a great photo with your blog post. If you don't have one on hand, you can purchase stock photos from web sites like BigStockPhoto.com or Shutterstock.com for a few dollars. Professional photos not only make your blog look more credible, but also help to draw attention to you when you promote your blog on other social networks like LinkedIn or Facebook. Posts with compelling photos get more clicks.

Your blog is also a potential source for reporters and bloggers writing about your topic. Today's journalists use the Internet to research and find ideas for their next story. The comments and interest of fans, followers and friends help journalists get an indication of interest in a particular story or topic. The more comments a topic has, the more likely the journalist will be to pursue that story. Therefore, optimizing your blog posts and social networking updates for keywords is essential for coming up in a journalist's research path.

If you'd rather not wait for the journalists to find you, you can also reach out to them. You can do this by determining the individual bloggers and journalists who may be interested in what you have to say and reaching out to each of them with a brief description of what you've written along with why their readers would be interested. This is the basic time-tested "press release" style of attracting journalists and news coverage. It's important to do the leg work of actually reading the writer's past articles so that you don't pitch a story on the merits of bike lanes to the publication's business editor. Most blogs and some online news media will include the writer's email address with their posts or in a "contact us" section.

Online publications and blogs need content: a relevant tweet, a good project or blog post can be picked up by influential players —— amplifying and adding credibility to your message. Kenneth Caldwell[12], a San Francisco, California-based communications consultant for architecture and design firms, sends a customized pitch letter, a PDF of his clients' projects with images and no more than one page of text to a targeted list of bloggers and journalists. "Online press and social media make it possible to get a story out in a few days, as opposed to six-to-12 months that it takes with print publications."

---

12   www.kennethcaldwell.com

If you can't find a direct way to contact journalists through email, Twitter can be more effective in getting their attention. Search for the writer's name on Twitter and follow them. Then stay tuned. Listen to their tweets for an opening to contribute your own experience —then reply with something interesting. Once you have established a dialog with this person, you can suggest a story idea that is relevant to your area of expertise.

If your story warrants a broader appeal and you are looking for a way to broadcast your announcement to the social web, you may want to consider a hybrid of the traditional press release — the social media release (SMR). The SMR is basically the evolution of the original press release but speaks more plainly to the intended reader and provides organized access to relevant information sources from across the web. Reporters, bloggers and anyone else who finds its content interesting can incorporate one or more elements of it into a blog post, status update or tweet. A typical SMR may include a list of facts relating to the announcement, supporting quotes, downloadable images and multimedia files, links, related web pages as well as background information on the person or firm. All of these are keyword optimized, of course, as discussed previously. Ultimately an SMR is intended to appeal to traditional journalists as well as bloggers and consumers. The big press release distribution services like PRWeb and BussinessWire can optimize your press release for social media, but there are a handful of free services, like PitchEngine, Pressitt and PRX that can do this as well. However, the mass customized distribution of these tools is the downside. "Social media is not about connecting with untold thousands, it's about using technology to find and connect with your very focused constituencies. It's still about relationships," reminds Caldwell.

Self-promotion on Facebook and LinkedIn

We are seeing more and more corporate executives and entrepreneurs use their Facebook profiles to promote themselves personally, outside of the more corporate company Facebook page. The idea is to "make your business personal." In other words, the more you share your personal side with readers and Facebook friends, the stronger they will feel about your work. With that said, here are four ways to promote your personal profile page.

Update your Facebook page frequently, but not more than once per day.
Each time you update your site, that information becomes available to all your friends via the news feed feature. The news feed feature can even open your information up to your friends' friends and is most successful at taking information viral. Stay away from posting mundane things like what you had for lunch and instead post links, updates and information that are related to your brand and ideals. And always add a link to your latest blog post. It's also a good idea to include a question to get your friends to comment and engage. Facebook posts that gain the most comments stay at the top of the news feed longest and get the most exposure.

Upload visuals
Photos and videos help capture attention. And since design, and planning professions are visual industries, it is a great way to show what you do. Use colorful, casual, candid photos. It will help your profile stand out more in the news feeds as well as communicate a human element to your work. If you specialize in one area of your field, it's a good idea to post photos of yourself that help promote

that brand. For example, an engineer specializing in tunneling could post pictures of himself on the project site or next to the giant boring machinery to show the scale of the project.

Tag friends and post on walls

Tags* are links to another Facebook profile or page within a post. Not only does this create a link back to their page from your post, but Facebook also adds the post to the tagged friend's wall. To tag someone, type the "@" sign before typing their name (without a space between the two) and Facebook will suggest a list of friends, pages and causes for you select from. SWA Group tagged one of their famous clients in a post about an op-ed they had written, "California Academy of Sciences Green Roof: Three Years Later". The tag automatically added the post to the California Academy's Facebook page and notified the tagged page Admin about the mention. As a result, the Admin commented on the SWA post which then appeared in the newsfeed of their 35,000+ fans. You can also use the "Write Post" feature to write directly on a friend's wall. When you write or post a comment on a friend's wall, all of their friends who visit the wall see it. This brings more attention to your profile and potential to link up with new fans. Seek out other industry friend" where your services don't necessarily compete. Work together to build great ideas that you can share with both of your Facebook friend bases.

Join targeted groups and causes

Joining specific Facebook groups and causes that align with your thought leadership mission (for example sustainability or green movements) opens you and your work up to more networks and potential friends. Post something on the wall of that group that provides real value and gets conversations going. This will help draw attention to your own Facebook profile.

Similarly, LinkedIn is a hotbed of group discussion activity for professionals. Depending on your area of interest, there are numerous organizations and client communities that you can join. "I've noticed, [online] places where architects' and engineers' clients play — Society for College and University Planning (SCUP) if you're in education, the Urban Land Institute (ULI) if you work for developers, Center for Health Design if you are in healthcare," states Chris Parsons of Knowledge Architecture. "They are blogging. They have LinkedIn groups and they are on Twitter. It's one thing to start your own thing, but it's another to go into [the clients'] environments and start commenting, sharing, tweeting and connecting about what they are interested in. It's low hanging fruit. These groups are really open and they are looking for feedback. What a great way for a senior designer or engineer to establish credibility and connect with clients through their blogs and social media efforts," observes Parsons.

Managing your time on the social web

The great thing about being a published author or public speaker is that you already have a wealth of information to pull from. You can edit excerpts from your book, articles and presentations and turn them into valuable blog posts. This has a danger of becoming quite time-consuming. Marcela Abadi Rhoads, author of the ADA Companion Guide, estimates she spends about 10 hours per week on social networking activities. Rhoads says she posts something to a

Ideas for your Social Media Content

PRESENTATIONS & ARTICLES
Create a blog series about your topic
Focus each post on one point

BOOK
Chapter excerpt from your book
'Uncut' interviews from your sources
Review a related book or article

COMMENTARY OR PERSONAL PERSPECTIVE
Industry trend
Body of research
Book, article, or presentation
Project

PROJECTS: YOUR OWN & YOUR PEERS
To illustrate your point
Before and after
Photo essays
Discipline trends

YOUR OWN RESEARCH OR FINDINGS
Illustrate as infographic
Use project related research
Join the conversation about other people's findings

OTHER SOURCES
Collect third party content on your topics
Feature another blogger's topic related post
Invite guest bloggers
Surprise readers by writing something
slightly off-topic

site of her own and comments on another person's site every day to help establish herself as an expert. Sometimes she will post original content, while other times she will post a link to a helpful article she found.

If you can manage it, participating on social networking sites once a day is a great way to stay in the conversations. However, you can also be quite effective with a once-a-week post — as long as that one post is of high quality and gets long-lasting conversations going. Another strategy we recommend for our busy clients is to spend one to two months posting many things, many times, on various social networks at various times of day. Then closely monitor the results so you can identify the best times, places and frequency to participate for maximum impact. (We'll show you how to track all of these things in Chapter 7.)

Another strategy for time-efficient participation is regular use of the social listening tools such as Radian6, Google Alerts and others mentioned earlier previously. Participate in the moment when you find a conversation happening online that you can contribute valuable insight to. This helps keep your social networking time extremely targeted.

Although custom content creation is ideal for establishing yourself as a thought leader, doing so can be labor and time-intensive. Fortunately, you don't always have to create every post from scratch. Save time by posting a link to an important article or industry trend and provide your own commentary. Professional magazines for your particular field of study offer hundreds of possible topics each month to assist you in this short-cut. But don't repeat the article's point; simply glean ideas from the articles to help you save time.

Content sharing, or simply posting a link on your social networks to compelling information that someone else wrote is another easy way to generate fresh posts. Finding and sharing essential industry information can prove to consumers that your firm understands the industry and has a genuine interest in wanting to help others in the industry keep informed on important trends. Plus, by posting a colleague's article to your social network, you are showing support of their ideas. Your colleague will possibly be more interested in posting your later article on their own social network in return.

Make your social profile the hub for all information centered around your subject expertise by providing an easy way for your fans and followers to find the information they need and keep up-to-date on important trends and topics they care about. Make it the first and final source potential clients and colleagues can come for information.

We are seeing more and more professionals engage in content-sharing activities as a way to generate fresh posts and establish themselves as an individual with a handle on the pulse of the industry. In fact, this strategy of content-sharing is now being used by nearly half of all U.S. marketing professionals; according to February 2011 research from the content curation firm HiveFire[13], more than 75% of those marketing professionals engage in content curation for the primary purposes of establishing themselves as thought leaders and elevating brand visibility and buzz.

---

13   http://www.getcurata.com

Ultimately, social media gives every person the chance to publish ideas and stand on their own soap box. But it seems the more information there is out there, the less able we are to understand it. If thought leadership is your goal, you need to find a way to capture your reader's attention — by doing something or saying something that is authentic and brave. But here's the catch: it has to be relevant. Read the brief side bar on how one relevant tweet was retweeted more than 8,000 times.

The power of a relevant re-tweet

Scenario: On March 10, 2011 when the news about the magnitude 8.9 earthquake in Honshu, Japan broke, Dave Ewing (@DaveEwing) located in Colorado had been watching videos of Tokyo that showed a city holding its own again the fifth largest earthquake in history. Meanwhile, #prayforJapan was trending on Twitter.

He sent out a tweet. **The headline you won't be reading: "Millions saved in Japan by good engineering and government building codes". But it's the truth.**

What happened: According to Ewing's "A Bit Freaked Out" blog post, "The next morning I noticed my iPhone was awake. It was showing notifications of retweets — at what looked like about once a second. Yikes! When I checked my email, I had more than 300 new followers on twitter. Eeak!" A couple of hours later, his tweet was the top news item on Reddit, a website that ranks the popularity of what's currently happening online.

We saw the tweet as a retweet, but hadn't realized the expanse of its impact until we read about its success in a ClickZ.asia blog post by Vijay Sankaran. By searching for key words in the tweet on Topsy, a search engine for social media, we learned that Dave Ewing's tweet was forwarded more than 8,300 times. This was possible because more than 750 of those were by "influential" people, meaning their messages strongly influence the actions of others. This includes the more than 50,000 followers of Andy Carvin, who is a senior strategist at NPR and the more than 200,000 followers of Philip DeFranco, the host of The Phillip DeFranco Show Mondays through Fridays on his YouTube channel that has more than 1.7 million subscribers. Sankaran estimates that Dave Ewing's late night message may have reached millions of Twitter users across the world.

Equally influential in spreading Ewing's message are the well-read bloggers that were inspired by his tweet. San Francisco-area blogger Josh Rosenau who writes for ScienceBlogs used Ewing's tweet as his headline and opening statement in a post that analyzed the severity and destruction of the quake. U.K. online tabloid Anorak featured Ewing's tweet as an alternative perspective. "Japan Earthquake news headlines focus on the doom. But what about the wonder of humanity that created buildings able to withstand a tsunami? ... What about thinking how much worse it would have been without human ingenuity?" A blogger in Amman, Jordan referenced the success of Ewing's tweet as the motivation for writing his post about earthquake preparedness. Prolific bloggers look for content ideas everywhere.

Why: At a time when people were looking for spiritual explanations and support, Dave Ewing drew the world's attention to the heroes of the crisis — engineers and building codes — all in 132 characters. By saying something different from everyone else, Ewing connected with people who were hungry for an optimistic point of view and eager to share it. (Although, he now wishes he'd said government regulation instead of building codes.)

Resources:
@DaveEwing
http://www.ewingdev.com/blog/

www.topsy.com	www.reddit.com
@acarvin	@PhillyD
www.youtube.com/sxephil#p	scienceblogs.com
www.anorak.co.uk	blog.ambitious.me

Chapter 6
Building and Nurturing Communities

By now, you should have narrowed in on your core business and marketing goals, identified your firm's key influencers and/or potential thought leaders, and focused in on where and how your target audience engages online. Now, it's time to build your online community.

An online community is a place where like-minded individuals come together to share, learn and exchange ideas with the use of Internet-based tools. Therefore, your online community can live within any of the popular social networking sites such as a designated Twitter hashtag, a LinkedIn group, Facebook page or as a sub-group within an already existing online community in the A/E industry. You can also create and customize your own community outside these existing groups in the form of a blog, forum or message board. With today's web tools, you can even set up an entire social networking site for your firm, without having to know any web programming. When you understand your target audience, along with your overall goals for growing your community, you can identify which Internet tools provide the best solutions for creating your online community. In some cases, you may choose multiple online platforms to develop your community.

For Steve Mouzon social media was the natural next step for his already active offline community. Mouzon founded the New Urban Guild in 2001. Pre-social media, the Guild would organize workshops, piggybacking on events held by organizations that appreciated what the New Urban Guild was doing, like Restore Media in Washington, D.C. which publishes magazines and hosts events for the traditional building market. The events were the source of real value for the guild because that's where workshop attendees could learn from each other, share experiences and develop real relationships with one another. Social media has allowed the guild to communicate multi-directionally — like they used to at events — at any time.

Social Media also allowed Mouzon to engage a larger group. He now regularly interacts with his community through his "Useful Stuff" blog[1], and also on Twitter and Facebook. Mouzon also launched "The Original Green," an initiative to resurrect the sustainable principles that were inherent in all architectural and engineering design before the thermostat age. The Original Green is most active on Facebook with more than 1,000 fans, but it also has a more conversant, albeit much smaller, community on LinkedIn.

Whichever platform you decide to use to build your online community, the crucial element is this: your community must have a clear purpose that your target audience cares about. Don't try to create a purpose. Instead, build off a purpose that many people are already passionate about and are already talking about.

The American Institute of Architects (AIA) found unexpected success in building a loyal online community base when they launched a Twitter chat. Followers simply used hashtag #aiachat to join a range of conversations of interest to fellow architects including sustainability, green design, design's influence on K-12 education, client relationships and more. AIA chat began as a simple feature of National Architecture Week in 2010 and quickly grew from there. Although the conversations were lead by the AIA, anyone could join in the conversation.

"I was overwhelmed at the participation rate and level of interaction [of the first AIA Chat on Twitter]," says Sybil Walker Barnes, director of social media for the AIA[2] in Washington, D.C. "We had nearly

---

1 http://usefulstuff.posterous.com/
2 www.aia.org

100 commenters take part in the initial chat, not counting those who simply observed.

"More importantly," she continues, "I received a lot of feedback requesting to continue the conversation. It almost seemed as if our members and followers were looking for a community or a way to connect on Twitter. I had a lot of fun with the chat; they didn't have to twist my arm to continue it. I enjoy seeing the interactions among users during the chats and camaraderie that is developing among some of them that wasn't apparent prior to the chats.

"Since the initial chat, AIA chat has continued monthly on the first Wednesdays of the month at 2 p.m. Eastern Time on Twitter. Last fall we extended it from 60 minutes to a 90-minute chat, again based on feedback. Even at the end of 90 minutes, some participants continue amongst themselves," explains Barnes.

AIA chat on Twitter is only one of the many social media channels the AIA is using to connect with their members who are congregating in social forums online. The AIA also uses LinkedIn and Facebook as well as their own social site, KnowledgeNet. The AIA's online success seems to lie in the use of technology that their target audience feels most comfortable interacting with.

AIA Case Study: Social Communities

The American Institute of Architects (AIA) has more than 84,000 registered members and an untold number of non-members who follow the organization as an authority on the profession.

Sybil Walker Barnes shares how the AIA is using social media to connect with and unite both of these groups.

Testimonial: Interview with Sybil Walker Barnes, Washington, D.C.-based AIA director of social media) regarding the organization's online community of architects.

Objective: We want to primarily connect with AIA members who are online but we also know that many of our followers and fans are not members. Given the economic challenges the architecture profession is facing, we know that our social channels are, for some, their only means of keeping their professional tie to the AIA. For both members and nonmembers, we want to become a trusted source of news and information for and about the architecture profession. We want to be the source for all things architecture.

Strategy:
Early on we recognized that the millions of online conversations taking place daily are a data mine for us so our strategy is threefold:

1. **Go where our members are:** We know that there is a subgroup of our members who are using social networks. We want to be there for them and with them because we know that a virtual presence can sometimes translate to a real-world opportunity.

2. **Listen:** Around 2008 we started seeing mentions of the AIA online and we began thinking about how we can better listen to

them and apply the information we hear, both positive and negative, to our programs, products and services. The social channels enable us to listen easily to our members and prospects.

3. **Engage with our members and prospects:** Engagement is key for us. We want to use the social channels and take a humanized approach to our use of social media. In essence, we want to put a face, or faces, behind the AIA. We want users to know who we are and to readily identify with us.

We informally launched our social media program testing members' reception to our members-only LinkedIn group. Because of its favorable reception and steady growth, we then set up a Facebook group. That, too, was well received. But we began to wonder if perhaps a closed group limited our reach. In 2009 we experimented with a Facebook fan page and Twitter account, both open to all. Based on their constant growth, in January 2010 we officially launched the AIA Social Media Program and designated a director of social media (me), who has oversight of the program.

We currently have a presence on LinkedIn, Twitter, Facebook, YouTube, and Flickr. We also have our own social site, KnowledgeNet. And we [recently launched] our page on Foursquare.

Each of the social sites has a different flavor and we wanted to use the advantages of each to create a community.

Through our LinkedIn group, members connect with each other and share their thoughts, experiences, concerns and queries. It's truly professional networking at its best. Rather than interrupt the member-to-member conversations, we let members connect with each other in the foreground and we use regularly scheduled LinkedIn updates as our back channel to communicate news to members.

We set up the AIA National YouTube channel early-on in AIA presence in social media to serve as a repository for our video presentations.

One of our fastest-growing sites is our Facebook fan page. Here, fans not only receive the latest news and information about the architecture profession and the AIA but also updates that serve to engage them in dialogue with each other. I'm hoping to grow our efforts on the fan page this year and include more links to some of our most popular landing pages on aia.org and present a more integrated presentation with our official magazine, Architect.

Twitter is our micro-blogging site, providing quick, short updates about the AIA and the profession. Building a community presents a bit of a challenge on Twitter, though.

Our strategy for using each begins by assessing whether the content we're linking to on the social sites relates to our vision and mission. If it does, then we assess whether we want comments/feedback. If we do, then we post to a blog, Facebook, or LinkedIn. If it's something we're not setting out

AIA presence

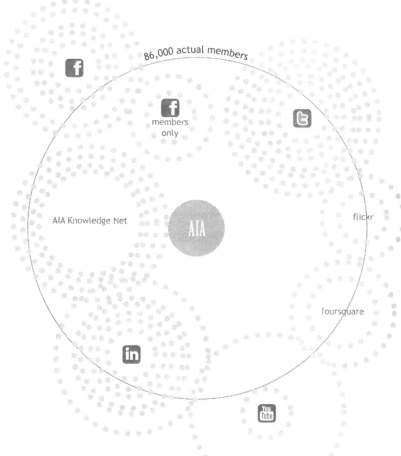

86,000 actual members

members only

AIA Knowledge Net

AIA

flickr

foursquare

to engage them with, then it's posted to Twitter, Facebook, or YouTube if appropriate.

Our focus is on building community and connecting members who are online. Everything that we do on the social networking channels is to help users connect with each other and facilitate their online discussions. That means we do things like host live twitter chats monthly, host a virtual National Architecture Week observance, feature ways for members to connect with us and each other at our national convention, sponsor a virtual convention, to name a few. Also, we signal the importance we place on our social media efforts by keeping our social media networks in the forefront, such as a social icon bar on the homepage and footer of our website and email signature blocks emphasizing social media sites.

Resources:
www.aia.org
network.aia.org/Home
www.facebook.com/AIANational
www.facebook.com/group.php?gid=4704710411 (or search for "AIA Members")
@AIANational
www.youtube.com/user/AIANational
foursquare.com/aianational
http://www.linkedin.com/groups?home=&gid=113822&trk=ane t_ug_hm&goback=.gdr_1321671078484_1

Key benefits of building an online community

By developing and managing an active online community around your firm's core values and strengths, your firm then becomes a leader in your chosen area and as we show below, your members help to spread your firm's mission. Masco Cabinetry in Ann Arbor, Michigan may sell most of its products directly to consumers, but the company recognizes the influence of product recommendations and project specifications from members of the design profession. Director of Architect Relations and Education Mark Johnson, FAIA, was hired to build a community of architects, interior designers, custom builders and remodelers — segments beyond the traditional kitchen and bath industry, that Masco had never reached before.

Chris Parsons — add new contact to email marketing list — connect to new contact personally — invite new contact to KA Connect Community

KA Connect: Process for Community Management

Twitter is Johnson's network of choice. He does have a presence on Facebook and LinkedIn to reach those who want to follow his messages but aren't on Twitter. While we don't advise replicating the same posts on each of your networks — for Johnson it is the key to the reach of his message. Johnson explains, "Because of time constraints, the only way to develop content for multiple social media sites was to use a tool to aggregate, in my case Hootsuite." He acknowledges that tweets can be "cryptic" on other platforms, the 140 character limit makes Twitter his preferred platform for communicating and engaging quickly. "I've found that a relevant tweet to a relevant following can translate into significant click-throughs. With 3,000 followers, I can drive 50-90 click-throughs with a single tweet."

Managing an online community also gives you the opportunity to understand first-hand the needs of your target audience and/or industry based on member comments within the community. As a result, you can better position your firm to develop solutions to core desires and problems. In the end, building an online community will help you to become a better company.

Building your own social networking site

We remember a time not too long ago when the cost to develop your own social networking site was upwards of half a million dollars in programming fees alone. Today, you can get a social networking site launched for as little as $19 per month and you don't have to know a thing about programming. Websites like Ning[3] allow you to set up a full social networking site with all the core community features such as forums, blogs and various widgets to help you reach your goals. You can even choose the colors and layout of your social network to match your firm's existing website or marketing materials. Ning also provides an easy "single sign-on" option, which allows people to use their Facebook, Google or other social networking site

---

3   www.ning.com

login to join your community. Allowing members to use existing social profiles to log in makes the barrier to entry even easier.

Forums or message boards are perhaps the oldest form of social networking and remain a core function of most online communities. Internet users participated in forums long before Facebook or blogs even existed, and they survived for a reason: they are easy to use and they work. Forums give members an easy way to ask questions and share ideas. They also provide lots of great keyword-friendly text and links that search engines love. The more activity your forums have around a particular topic or industry question, the more likely your forum will show up on top of the search engines.

While there are several do-it-yourself forum options available, bigger firms hoping to grow a larger community may want to consider hiring a company such as Lithium[4]. Lithium is a California-based company that can help you customize a community forum that will also tie into popular social networks such as Twitter and Facebook. An added benefit to hiring a full service company like Lithium over a do-it-yourself service like Ning is access to services such as 24/7 moderation. Such a service can be an important time-saver if you don't have extra staff on-hand to regularly check into a fast-growing community. We found that using a full-service company's moderators like the ones provided by Lithium was critical while setting up Verizon's online community. Thousands of members and hundreds of posts were made within the online community on a daily basis. Outside moderators helped Verizon's internal staff identify both potential problems as well as influential members who could keep the community running.

---

4   www.lithium.com

For Verizon, influential community members are the ones who not only made frequent posts but made quality contributions that gave the community as a whole value. Because Verizon's online community is designed to function as a peer-to-peer technical support forum, quality posts by influential members was the lifeblood of keeping the community a success. Therefore, to keep customers on the community forums and away from expensive customer support phone calls, it was vital to keep these influential members happy and continuing to post technical help to other customers. Some ways Verizon kept these community influences happy was by acknowledging them publically on blogs, giving them direct access to community managers and moderators and awarding them special badges and icons to use with their online profiles.

While few A/E firms will be able to generate a community as big or as active as Verizon's, the roles of moderator, community manger and core influencers are vitally important and worth the time investment required to help grow and manage a vibrant online community. "The first four months on Twitter, I averaged three to four hours per day, seven days a week, much of it on my own time," notes Mark Johnson speaking about the amount of time he invested in building his community. "To continue growing a community and engaging followers takes at least an hour a day, better if I can devote two hours per day."

If you can't dedicate a resource to this in your company we recommend that A/E firms consider outsourcing moderation and/or a community manager role so that the day-to-day management requirements don't prevent your online community from thriving.

Designating a community manager

In a perfect world, your community members would keep conversations buzzing and topics tasteful. However, in the real world, online communities don't run themselves. If you want to keep your online community on track and consistently reflecting your firm's missions, values and business goals, you need to designate a community manager. That community manager can be your marketing director or an Internet marketing consultant who specializes in community management. Whoever you designate, it must be someone who understands the reasons you set up this community in the first place and will adhere to your company's social media guidelines (as discussed in chapter 4).

Your community manger must also care about the growth of your community and its members. Knowledge Architecture created a community around its annual event, KA Connect. The community is nurtured by the firm founder Chris Parsons and is truly a labor of love. Especially at the beginning, community managers like Parsons aren't just shepherding conversations by responding to posts and comments. They are privately encouraging members to post new content. It's the community manager's responsibility to facilitate content, dialogue and a positive atmosphere in the community that encourages members to participate.

KA Connect Case Study

Firm: Knowledge Architecture (KA), San Francisco, California

Challenge: Chris Parsons launched KA in 2009 with a software solution to help medium-to-large architecture and engineering firms make the most of their data, knowledge and expertise. His frustration, as a former in-house IT leader, was that the discussions about knowledge management tended to focus on people talking about BIM and technology infrastructure. Parsons believed that in order for KA to be successful, he needed to move the conversation toward information and away from technology. If he were to be successful at selling knowledge management, he needed to expand his audience from the CIO and IT staff to include marketing and operations managers discussing these concepts.

With his company only four months old, Parsons announced to his LinkedIn connections that he was going to host an event called KA Connect to define "knowledge management" through applied examples. Then he built a website and a blog to help promote the event. The 2010 event was held in Chicago and featured a PechaKucha 20 x 20 format to start to define "knowledge management." Parsons lined up about 15 speakers of various disciplines and he expected 25-to-30 people to show up as attendees. To his surprise, more than 80 people came. The event did more than share success stories. The interactive format led to conversations, debates and new ideas. According to Parsons, "At the end of the event, it felt like we were just getting started."

KA Connect: Keeping Conversations Fresh

In person dialog results in question or comment that could be a good discussion starter within the community

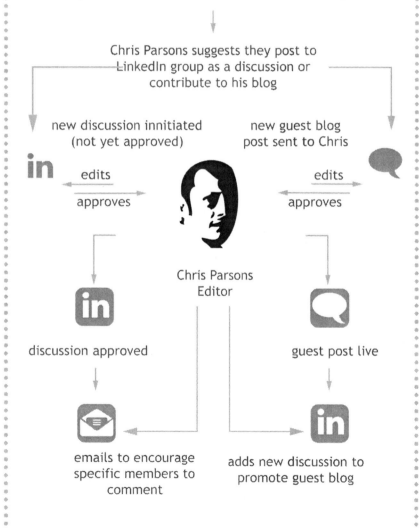

Chris Parsons suggests they post to LinkedIn group as a discussion or contribute to his blog

new discussion innitiated (not yet approved)

new guest blog post sent to Chris

edits

approves

edits

approves

Chris Parsons
Editor

discussion approved

guest post live

emails to encourage specific members to comment

adds new discussion to promote guest blog

<<Sidebar: Originating in Tokyo in 2003 by two young architects, PechaKucha networking events, or "20 x 20's" take place in many cities small and large around the world. The PechaKucha format is a short presentation of a singular idea, 20 slides that are automatically advanced every 20 seconds for a total presentation time of 6 minutes, 40 seconds. At the end of the 6 minutes 40 seconds another presenter takes the stage. The concise, fast-paced format allows ideas to be exchanged rapidly and opens up time and attention for discussion.>>

Objective: To capture the momentum started by the event and continue the conversations in a new forum.

Strategy: The day after the event, Parsons sent an email to all who attended the event and to those who expressed interest in attending but couldn't make it, to announce a new KA Connect Group on LinkedIn. Within days, members were posing questions — both practical and philosophical — to the group and getting thoughtful responses. This was not without effort on the part of Parsons though.

As manager of the group, Parsons is heavily involved. Parsons developed a three-step regimen, as shown in figure 6.2, that he follows each time he is introduced to someone or accepts their business card:

1. Add their name to the KA email marketing list.
2. Personally connect with them on LinkedIn.
3. Invite this person to join the KA Connect LinkedIn group.

Through his diligence in growing the community and through grass roots referrals from members, the group has grown steadily from that first day.

The KA Connect Group is a closed group, so people have to be accepted to the group to become a member. When Parsons receives a request to join, he sends a personalized welcome letter to each new member. While the same information is shared in each letter, he tailors the message to what he knows about this person. Parsons also uses this initial communication to get feedback from them by asking what they are interested in learning and how they found out about the group.

The KA Connect content is mostly contributed by others in the group but Parsons' fingerprints are all over them. Every new discussion passes through him before it is posted and often Parsons will respond privately to the initiator with some minor editorial tweaks or suggestions to make the post more likely to ignite a response from other members before he approves it. Sometimes he is involved even before this. Parsons shared an example with us of a simple phone conversation with one of the 2011 KA Connect presenters during the lead-up to the event, "he asked for a suggestion about working within the 20 slides x 20 seconds format. So instead of telling him what I thought, I asked him to query the group." But Parsons doesn't stop there. He also actively solicits discussion. Parsons regularly emails KA Connect members when he sees a connection between their personal work/interests and a conversation thread to suggest that they contribute their point of view. He draws a line at editing comments so that these can be spontaneous and change course as conversations naturally do — with the exception of the very rare personal attacks, which he removes completely.

Parsons also uses the LinkedIn group to generate responses and/or start a new discussion about something that has been added to the KA Connect blog or website. For example, after the 2010 live KA Connect event, Parsons posted the videos of each presentation to the event's website and to iTunes. Periodically, he would start a new discussion that features a key point from one of the presentations, noting (and linking to) the recording, and posing a related question to the group. On the KA Connect blog, guest blog entries often originate in the same way as the discussions threads — as a result of something someone said to Parsons in person, on the phone or in an email. Parsons stops them after they've made an interesting point and asks them to write a blog post on the topic and then follows up later to remind them that he is still interested.

Results: In July 2011 the KA Connect Group on LinkedIn amassed more than 1,000 members. By our estimation, two-to-three new discussions are started each week. Almost all of these generate a few comments from group members, some generate upwards of 20 to 60 comments. Discussions sometimes stay active for months — thanks in part to LinkedIn's group digests and opt-in automated emails that notify you when someone replies to a discussion that you have commented on or liked.

There were also twice as many attendees at the second annual KA Connect event in 2011.

Beyond the statistics, Parsons will tell you that the discussions that take place here are also helpful to his business. Points that are made here help him refine his perspective on these topics. The group is also a resource that he turns to with his own questions.

Lessons: Community and the degree of comfort needed in an environment where people openly share ideas and offer feedback, is something that KA works to create inside its client organizations. Parsons attributes much of the success of KA Connect to its in-person start. In fact, he often advises his clients to physically bring people together — even just once every couple of years — as a way of making internal communications tools more effective. While most of its members have not attended either of the KA Connect real world events, those who have attended are the most active in the forum. The result is a genuine feeling of camaraderie and willingness to help one another.

It's still about relationships. Find ways to bring your community together in the real world to breathe new life into your circle and to strengthen the connections between individuals.

Resources:
http://knowledge-architecture.com/
http://www.ka-connect.com/
http://www.linkedin.com/groups?home=&gid=2952414&trk=anet_ug_hm
http://twitter.com/karchitecture
http://www.facebook.com/pages/KA-Connect/114305828595366

For firms operating globally, community managers need to have the authority to take action, under set guidelines, should a heated online debate happen within your community in the middle of the night. Sometimes a single negative post within your community that remains unmanaged can spread like a virus, generating many comments during the wee hours of the morning. By the time you roll into the office and begin to address the problem, the damage is already done. According to a 2011 survey sponsored by Symantec and performed by Applied Research[5], the most common type of damage due to a social media mishap is lowering consumer trust in your company and brand. The survey included enterprises with 1,000 or more employees and found that 28% reported damage to brand reputation or loss of customer trust due to a specific negative social media post. The average estimated cost of that damage: $638,496. This statistic is not meant to deter you from using social media in your marketing arsenal but to emphasize the importance of employee training in social media and assigning a trusted community manager. Having a designated manager responsible for monitoring the community at all times is an important piece of controlling the direction of your community's voice and limiting possible damages that can occur to your company's brand. The tools you use to build your community and how you choose to manage it are important considerations. However, even more vital to your community's success will be the influence of its core members.

---

5   http://www.informationweek.com/thebrainyard/news/industry_analysis/231002459/could-social-media-flub-cost-you-43-million

Online communities need loyal members

A key ingredient to online community success is the passion and loyalty of the members. Without your members, you have no followers, no fans, no key influencers, no one engaging with your ideas and no one looking to you as a leader in your field; in other words, no community. Nurturing and building an online community comes after you have a marketing plan in place to let potential followers know about the benefits of joining your community.

Building up a community may come quicker for those A/E firms who already have a strong offline following, especially for firms who also have a well-known mission or brand tied to a strong social purpose or cause. These firms can further expand their industry influence by channeling ideas into an online community where they can watch followers expand on ideas and help them flourish. This is certainly Mark Johnson's strategy. Johnson is developing a design blog on the Masco Cabinetry website. "Hopefully, my existing followers will help me build a new blog following much faster than starting from scratch," says Johnson.

With today's cost-effective social tools and viral nature of the web, even an individual, a smaller or lesser known firm in the A/E industry can develop a loyal online community following. Johnson suggests becoming a content aggregator. "You can't be an expert in everything and the experts appreciate you pointing others to their content to help build their following." Johnson publishes 25 to 30 e-newspapers five days a week on topics ranging from 3D rendering to social media. "I'm aggregating the expert content from many others into a single topic e-newspaper which is probably faster than users doing web searches on their own."

Whether you are a large, well-know firm or a smaller consultancy, the following list of action items can encourage membership in your online community.

Invite members to join

When you are ready to launch your new online community, personally invite contacts who would contribute or benefit from the community. Send a personal email inviting your close contacts to be among the first members. This will give you a chance to get honest feedback on content as well as generate membership, comments and activity before you announce your community to the world.

Make your first members feel important. Request that they introduce themselves to each other. Seed valuable content and give new members clear actions to take. For example, ask for their feedback on a specific blog post or forum topic. By making them feel a part of the community, they are more likely to contribute and recommend it to their peers.

Announce your community to your target audience

In Chapter 2, we discussed ways to find your target audience. As you join and listen in on existing groups your audience is participating in, take time to make insightful and valuable comments or offer solutions to problems or questions. Then at the end of your comment, let members know that your firm recently started a community around this exact topic, and offer the direct link if they'd like to join.

Let members know how they can contribute to the community. An often overlooked but still powerful tool for encouraging engagement of new members is the "welcome email." Depending on what tool you use to build your online community, you can set up an automatically generated email that thanks members for joining and confirms their registration with your community. Many community managers might leave the welcome email at that, but you can benefit from taking this email a step further. After all, this is your first engagement with a new member. It's a critical point when the member will decide whether or not he or she wants to become more active in your community.

In your welcome email, provide links to your best content areas and active discussions. As your community evolves, so will your welcome email. It's also beneficial to provide new members with a direct link to where they can introduce themselves and either ask a question or make a comment about why they joined. Sometimes, entering a close-knit community of industry professionals and peers can feel intimidating to the new member. You want to encourage them to introduce themselves to the group and become part of the conversation.

Center your community on them, not you
This skill can require a soft-sell. You never want to use your community to push your business. Readers will likely get turned off very fast to the overt self-serving nature of this mistaken approach. Rather, use your community as a tool to build relationships with your target audiences and position your company as a leader in the industry. If members want to know exact services you provide or how to contact someone, they can easily find your website. Your

community should focus on providing genuine, valuable content that matters to your members and that reflects your company's overall marketing and business goals. The sales will follow.

Another way to make your community feel member-centered is to acknowledge and refer to influential members often. Consider interviewing members and incorporating their feedback into a weekly blog post. The more you show that you value your community member's input, the more likely they will continue to participate.

Take time to reward and build personal relationships with your top members

"Community Leader" is a term used to describe the most active and influential members of an online community. Many times, these community leaders will end up gaining more respect and authority within a community than the person who built the online community to begin with. It is essential that you build relationships with these powerful members for several reasons. Firstly, you want to remain equally potent in the community in comparison to these leaders. Also, a happy community leader can become one of your company's most powerful online advocates on and away from your community. But an unhappy community leader can do a lot of damage to your brand.

Rewarding community leaders for their participation and contribution is a great way to show your appreciation and encourage them to continue to engage. Rewarding members does not necessarily mean giving them free stuff. You can reward community leaders by simply recognizing them and acknowledging their contributions. You can also make them feel special by inviting them to participate in smaller groups of discussion or be the first to comment on a new project. For example, take the top five to 10 members in your community and let them be the first to learn about a new project you are working on and invite them comment on the new project.

Another way you can reward community leaders is to recognize that they have lives outside of your community. Reward influential members by interviewing them and highlighting their work as it relates to your community's mission in your next blog post. Be sure to promote that member's blog, twitter handle or company website to show support for their business goals in return for helping yours.

Depending on the platform on which you've chosen to build your online community, you may have the ability to offer members special titles, avatars, badges or icons to reflect their particular involvement in the community. While working with Verizon, we had several levels of titles and avatars members could use to show their involvement. With each level of participation came added privileges, such as access to private message boards. Our most loyal and influential members received the Community Leader title and badge. This title was reserved for a select few based on how often they posted as well as the value of those contributions. In order to keep conversations fresh, we selected a new group of community leaders every six months. We found that once we awarded members with titles and special privileges, their positive participation grew and helped the community flourish. These community leaders were the first ones to step in and support the company on a heated debate or assist on a technical problem a customer was having. Sharing community duties with your top members makes more people feel as if they have a vested interest in the success and growth of your company. Therefore, they are more likely to promote, defend and help your community thrive.

Be flexible about conversations and topics

Social media is about what is happening now and if current events or a new trend in the industry happens, you want your community to be flexible enough to become the centerpiece of conversation around it. Being the "go-to" spot for your area of expertise is what makes your company a true leader in your field.

Listen to your community and let your community expand in a way that will encourage users to continue to contribute and share your firm's values. This often involves having the courage to let go of control of the content of your community. Let members post blog entries or start topics in your forum. Although your social media strategy needs a clear direction, goals and a plan, you need to stay flexible. True social media marketing includes the ability to be relevant, flexible and useful while developing a connection to your audience.

Let debates happen

Debates are an important (and sometimes fun) element of an online community. Members wouldn't be there if they didn't feel passionate about your topic. Let debates happen and watch them unfold among members. If debates aren't happening, identify controversial topics around your community's core mission and plant a seed. Lively conversations that encourage active participation by many members are vital to the success and longevity of your community.

Sometimes a controversial topic will pop up around your company or a project you are working on. Nobody likes to see negative posts about themselves — especially within their own community. Resist the urge to automatically delete anything negative about your company. Decide whether a negative post is a rant (where nothing can be done to solve the problem) or can be viewed as constructive criticism. After all, keeping posts that are not completely positive shows that this is a genuine community where people can truly say how they feel. It also keeps your target audience talking within your community rather than going somewhere else to criticize your company or latest project. Keeping the unhappy member within your community gives you a chance to state your side of the story and possibly win them back. Take time to address any negative comments or concerns and, if appropriate, solicit member feedback on how you can fix the problem. If, however, the negative comment is more of a rant than constructive criticism, skip down to the next section to learn how you can handle "trolls."

Take the opportunity to meet in-person
It's great to get to know people online, but when you have the chance, try to meet people in real-life. If many of your members are going to be at a certain conference or event, encourage or organize a meet-up. Get to know the community members beyond the topic of your community and you may find more things you have in common. Mark Johnson has organized well-attended "Tweetups" with his network at the National AIA conference and at the Kitchen and Bath Industry Show. Chris Parsons' community was born from an in-person event. His community members organized local get-togethers through the LinkedIn group. The better-acquainted people are with

each other the more willing they are to share their own experiences and offer input.

Protect your members (and yourself) from trolls

In the world of online communities, trolls are those people who exist merely to leave negative comments on your blog, message boards or any other place you allow them to sneer. Trolls are not customers with a serious grievance or industry experts providing constructive criticism. They are internet users who literally troll social sites and add negativity and rants that not only make a community owner's heart sink, but can also intimidate, influence and adversely affect every member of a community. It is the community manager's job to identify and handle these trolls so they don't overrun your community.

A typical first reaction to a troll bad-mouthing your company, staff or a project will be to delete the offending comment. Avoid deleting troll comments at all costs. Once you start deleting posts, your community starts sounding more like a PR statement and less like a genuine community where all ideas are shared. This is a quick path to destroying your status as a thought leader and becoming just another propaganda-pushing phony blog. And it is likely to get the troll to troll more. Keep in mind that in some cases you should delete the post. Such cases include blatant spam, use of derogatory language, threats or harassment of other members of your community. In these cases, deletion and even banning the troll from the community is typically justified. Having clear standards for what you will and will not tolerate will also make it easier to explain if the troll ever calls you out for deleting their offensive comment.

However, if it does not justify deletion or banning how do you react to a troll comment? First, take a deep breath and never respond emotionally or by attacking the member back. This will only fuel the criticism and get others charged up to join the troll's battle. Instead, show you are listening and that you appreciate them taking the time to express their concern. In other words, "kill them with kindness." Your best-case scenario is that some of your loyal community members will jump to your defense and quiet the troll. And yes, it is acceptable to privately email your community leaders and encourage them to post a response to the troll's negative comment — just don't suggest what they should say. The last thing you need is for it to come out that you are trying to orchestrate a specific response.

The fact is that, despite their nasty and loud voices, most trolls are quite insecure. And we have learned first-hand that when enough community members post positive things contradicting the troll, the troll will back down. We've also seen a troll back off merely by the public reply from an official representative of the firm being attacked. This is especially effective when the accusations made by the troll were exaggerated or false to begin with (and the troll knew it). Showing trolls that you not only have support but are listening and will publicly react to their comments can be enough to quench false accusations or pointless rants.

Overall, what is your best strategy to keep trolls away? Support your loyal members and encourage them to speak out and defend your company. Chances are they will say all the things you wish you could say.

Lack of participation in your community

So you've built a great community and populated it with though-provoking content. You've also reached out to your contacts and invited them to join. Why aren't you getting more comments and participation? One reason may be that you don't have enough traffic to begin with. You need a fair amount of traffic coming to your online community to warrant conversations. Especially since only 10% of a community's overall traffic can be expected to post anything. Most members prefer to merely watch and listen. What's more, of that 10% that will post something, only 1% will actually start a conversation. The other 9% will simply comment on other people's topics. This means that until you generate enough traffic to get conversations going, you will need to actively spark dialogue by posting questions and comments. In other words, members won't talk or contribute unless they see others doing so. So get some messages posted to encourage others to start talking.

One way to make your community appear more active is to grow it slowly. For example, don't start a community with too many simultaneous conversation topics or categories. It's better to have a few very active topics than too many with too few conversations. Start with broad topics and see where the conversations go. You should naturally be able to identify which additional categories or message board topics should be added later on.

The visual and functional simplicity of your site is important. If your site appears too complicated and unfocused, people will not contribute. Having too much information can be intimidating to the first-time member and can keep users from participating. Keep a feel for the pulse of your community by monitoring what topics are of most interest to them and expand areas and grow accordingly.

One final note on why you may not be getting contributions in your community. Members may simply think it's boring. Perhaps you've centered content too much around your company and not enough on what the members want or are interested in. Your community rules and guidelines may also be too strict, especially if you are moderating and editing comments too much and not letting passion and personality shine through.

Remember this: your community must be based on a topic that your target audience is passionate about. And passionate people want to be able to express themselves. If they feel their comments are getting filtered, overly-responded to by you, or your community is otherwise too controlled, they will go elsewhere. Build a community that lets your target audience share ideas and converse passionately and watch your online reputation thrive.

Chapter 7
Evaluation Strategies

You have deadlines to meet, projects to launch and new clients to pitch. You don't have time to devote endless hours to a social media plan that won't work. And you didn't dive into social media to win a popularity contest or to drive millions of viewers to your website. You are building a social media campaign around your firm's specific business and marketing goals, which you defined early on while reading this book. It is the cost and time required to attain these goals that will measure the success of your social media efforts.

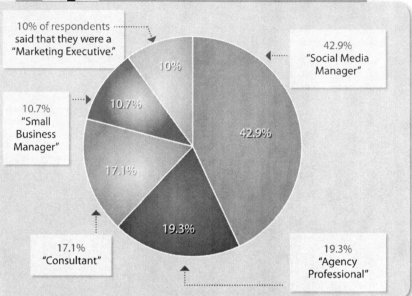

Who is buying SMM tools?
arranged by job title

10% of respondents said that they were a "Marketing Executive."

10%

42.9% "Social Media Manager"

10.7% "Small Business Manager"

10.7%

42.9%

17.1%

17.1% "Consultant"

19.3%

19.3% "Agency Professional"

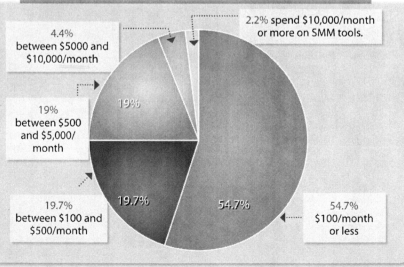

How much do people pay for SMM tools?

4.4% between $5000 and $10,000/month

2.2% spend $10,000/month or more on SMM tools.

19% between $500 and $5,000/month

19%

19.7% between $100 and $500/month

19.7%

54.7%

54.7% $100/month or less

Unlike tracking traditional online marketing activities such as sending email newsletters, analyzing ad buys and monitoring website traffic, social media campaign measurement can be a bit more elusive, mainly because it's about more than views, clicks and conversions.

Most digital metrics center around the beginning and end of the online relationships process. In other words, the first moment someone visits your website (view, click) and then the final act of becoming a lead (frequency of conversion). Social media falls somewhere in the center of this process and can be measured by engagement and interaction. When nurtured and implemented correctly, the strength of that engagement and quality of interaction will help a potential client or journalist form their ultimate decision about your company or you. It is these ongoing social interactions that help your connections ultimately decide whether they want to do business with you one time, multiple times or, in a best-case scenario, become a repeat customer and an online advocate for you and your firm.

Social media measurement, therefore, goes well beyond the first or even final click. It encompasses how groups of people are engaging with you, your firm and your employee thought leaders within social networks, and if those interactions are helping you reach your ultimate goal.

"Social media click-counting is for people trying to impress their bosses or hold onto their jobs," explains Scott Doyon, principal

Infographic courtesy of KISSmetrics Web Analytics (www.KISSmetrics.com) in partnership with OneForty (www.oneforty.com)

and director of marketing in Atlanta, Georgia at PlaceMakers, LLC. "It's not that I'm against the value of benchmarks and measuring, and it does help us understand where we're getting traction among our topics and initiatives, but our greatest focus is on the relationships we're developing and the evaluation of which ones emerge from and transcended the looser realm of social media, where there's little expectation of meaningful commitment, to become solid business opportunities."

PlaceMakers' goal for social media is to create meaningful, lasting relationships with people who may eventually become their clients, business partners or valued media connections. It is not about how many Twitter followers they can collect or even about attracting massive visitors to comment on their most recent blog post, but rather about the quality of engagement they receive as a result of their participation in social networks. It's about building real relationships that will lead to real opportunities.

Defining the health of your online community

Lithium Technologies is a firm that develops social media technologies and online communities for corporations. They've developed a way to predict the success of a growing social network. They call this measurement the "Community Health Index." This report goes beyond number of visits a community receives. It calculates the health of an online community by how well it meets the expectations and needs of the members.

Key attributes of a healthy, and therefore successful, community include:

Growth: increasing membership
Usefulness: great, relevant content
Popularity: overall importance in your industry
Responsiveness: how quickly members respond to questions and posts
Interactivity: how many members contribute at all
Liveliness: positive buzz and vibrancy a community and its members exude

At first glance, basing your measurement of community success on the happiness of your members can seem irrespective of your overall business goals. However, remember that social media success, especially in the A/E industries, is not just about one-time clicks and a quick sale. Building a lasting and useful social media presence takes time and patience. Building up a network where your target audience is happy and continues to participate will eventually help with your overall return on investment in your social media efforts. Your company will thrive with more professional respectability and higher sales volume if you have a strong social network.

The healthier your community becomes, the more likely your target audience will start to engage on your behalf and the less time you need to find members, develop new content and get conversations going. A thriving social network will help you market your services and gain access to new customers faster and is more cost-effectively than any other form of advertising today. When members start volunteering to help you by posting thoughtful, relevant content and recruiting new members themselves, it helps your bottom line in the fact that you can maintain a powerful social presence without necessarily having to be in the conversations every day. Even so, you'll still need a listening tool to keep track of what is being said about your company.

Tracking social listening

A powerful yet often-overlooked benefit of social media marketing is the ability to listen to conversations related to your business goals. There are many different levels and costs associated with listening tools. The most basic, and free tool, is Google Alerts, which we mentioned previously. Google Alerts works well for smaller companies without a huge web presence and offers a basic level of social listening. Simply go to google. com/alerts, provide your email address and some core keyword phrases including your company name and the names of your employee/company thought leaders and you will get an email alert each time these topics appear on the web. This will allow you to listen in and see what is being said about your people and your firm online; it can also be a good way to keep track of competitors.

For larger companies that are aggressively taking on social media, we suggest using a professional social listening tool such as Radian6. A Radian6 tool goes beyond Google Alerts by providing deeper analysis of conversations happening online.

A tool like Radian6 essentially helps you cut through the noise of social media and zero in on influential people talking about your company. This is ideal for busy professionals and firms that get a lot of media attention. Rather than having to read through every Google Alert that comes in, you can let the Radian6 dashboard advise you on which posts are most critical for you to respond to based on how much influence the person who posted the comment about your firm has. Finally, you can get a feel for the overall sentiment of Internet users in regard to your company, projects and industry and even look at comparisons as to how your company stacks up against your competitors.

Think of social media as the world's biggest focus group. By using listening tools you can discover what your target audience wants. This information can then be incorporated into your overall marketing strategy and help you reach your business goals as you deliver your services accurately to your customer.

While the above examples can help you monitor the overall health of your networks and listen to what is being said about your company, there are also many tools that let you track specific activities within your social networks, such as how friends and followers are reacting to your latest tweet or Facebook post. In these cases clicks and views can be important in helping you determine what types of content, as well as frequency, is of most interest to your audience so that you can take steps to build community health.

The best SMM tool?

What's the Best Social Media Monitoring Tool? It depends. Below is a brief list of tools at various price levels that may or may not be the best but are certainly among the most popular and capable social media monitoring tools currently available.

Tools more than $500 per month

Alterian SM2	socialmedia.alterian.com/products/sm2
Radian6	radian6.com
Cision	us.cision.com
Vocus	vocus.com
BrandChats	brandchats.com

what is "firehose access"?

When someone is given "firehose access" to a particular product, they are given access to a complete data stream, not just a sampling.

Tools less than $500 per month

UberVU	ubervu.com
Trackur	trakur.com
Beevolve	beevolve.com
SproutSocial	sproutsocial.com
SugarCRM	sugarcrm.com
Viral Heat	viralheat.com
HootSuite Pro	hootsuite.com/pro
Awareness Networks	awarenessnetworks.com
Argyle Social	argylesocial.com

Free tools

a tool that monitors social campaigns

- WildFire's Social Media Monitor

a tool that monitors upcoming events

- Plancast

tools that monitor with alerts

- Google Alerts
- BackType Alerts
- Yahoo Pipes
- Northern Light Search

tools that monitor comments & forums

- Comment Sniper
- coComment
- Board Reader
- Google Trends

tools that monitor social networks & blogs

- SocialMention
- Google Reader
- BlogPulse
- AllTop
- Google Realtime Search

a tool that monitors web page changes

- WatchThatPage

tools that monitor with social search

- Addict-o-matic
- Guzzle
- Social Seek
- BuzzFeed
- Buzzoo
- MonitorThis
- Alterian SM2 Freemium

tools that monitor twitter & facebook

- Seesmic
- Hootsuite
- Twitter Advanced Search
- Facebook Search
- Twitterverse Web Apps

twitterverse web apps

- Monitter
- TweetBeep
- Twazzup
- PostRank analytics
- Pulse of the Tweeters
- Twitscoop
- Twilert
- Sideline
- CoTweet
- PeerIndex
- MyTweeple
- MentionMap
- Twitterfall
- TweetMeme
- TweetDeck

Infographic courtesy of KISSmetrics Web Analytics (www.KISSmetrics.com) in partnership with OneForty (www.oneforty.com)

Many professionals in the A/E industry who are tracking their social media efforts are using a combination of tracking tools such as Hootsuite and Google Analytics[1].

"Even with its free level, Hootsuite offers so much for the user," says Deborah Reale, marketing specialist at Reed Construction Data, who uses the Hootsuite dashboard to monitor several social networking channels simultaneously, including Twitter, Facebook and LinkedIn. "Hootsuite gives analytics, which helps me identify our influencers."

Nick Bryan, public relations manager for HMC Architects uses a combination of several tracking tools including Google Analytics, Hootsuite and Chartbeat to monitor the success of HMC's social media efforts. "Hootsuite overlays HMC tweets with our website and blog traffic, thus connecting our tweets with website hits," explains Bryan.

Chartbeat is a subscription-based tool that shows you what is happening on your website or blog at that moment. "We are able to tell which tweets were popular and where users browsed after their initial click. [Using Chartbeat to understand] which pages on the web site are most popular gives our PR team insight as to which content is critical to keep fresh and updated," Bryan adds.

Mark Johnson of Masco Cabinetry checks on his Twitter progress with Hootsuite and unfollows people who haven't tweeted in a month or more and tests the number of click-throughs per tweet. He also uses the influence monitoring tool, Klout. Johnson checks

---

1   Google.com/analytics

out his Klout[2] score* and the scores of a few Twitter mentors to compare.

Google Analytics

Although there are plenty of robust, and possibly expensive, web analytics tools available, Google Analytics is an essential one that any A/E firm engaging in new media marketing must use. It's free, easy to set up, and, as you can see in the infographics, provides valuable information about your website's activity. Although Google Analytics will not show you the health and engagement of your social media efforts, it will show you what people who come from these social media channels eventually do when they finally visit your website. For example, do your Twitter followers fill out your "contact us" form and become quality leads? Do Facebook friends check out most pages of your online portfolio? Getting a sense for which online community drives the most desirable traffic to your site will help you determine which social network to invest effort in to reach your overall business and marketing goals.

When Lake Flato approached us to help them develop a social media marketing strategy, one of the first things we did was set up Google Analytics. By analyzing their current website's activity, we could quickly gauge which type of projects were of the most interest to current website visitors. This data can be used to help generate ideas of what topics can become the basis of content for a social media program.

---

2   www.klout.com

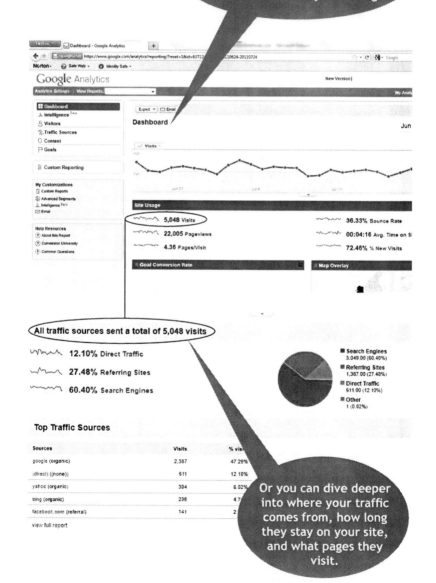

> The Google Analytics dashboard gives you a quick overview of your web site's traffic by date range.

All traffic sources sent a total of 5,048 visits

12.10% Direct Traffic

27.48% Referring Sites

60.40% Search Engines

■ Search Engines
3,049.00 (60.40%)

■ Referring Sites
1,387.00 (27.48%)

■ Direct Traffic
611.00 (12.10%)

■ Other
1 (0.02%)

Top Traffic Sources

Sources	Visits	% visi
google (organic)	2,387	47.29%
(direct) ((none))	611	12.10%
yahoo (organic)	304	6.02%
bing (organic)	238	4.7
facebook.com (referral)	141	2

view full report

> Or you can dive deeper into where your traffic comes from, how long they stay on your site, and what pages they visit.

Another important item we looked at was the bounce rate. In other words, when people got to the Lake Flato website, were they engaging with it or simply leaving ("bouncing") without visiting any other pages? Google Analytics showed us that in fact the Lake Flato website was engaging visitors and the site was therefore ready to capture the leads a well-considered social media strategy could deliver to the site. Work with an online marketing consultant and web developer to ensure your web site's bounce rate is around 30%. A bounce rate above 50% means you are losing more than half of your traffic, and your website may not yet be ready for social media campaign. If this is the case, call a web designer to help you re-tool your website so you can make the most impact from your social media efforts.

Google Analytics also provided insight into the keywords people were using on the search engines to find the Lake Flato website. From the keyword report, we discovered that more than 75% of Lake Flato's traffic was coming from people who already knew the company name. This shows strong name brand recognition and means there is a successful traditional PR and offline marketing effort. However, it also showed that they were missing a large portion of un-branded search terms. This means they were missing out on a significant amount of traffic from people searching for high quality, sustainable architecture services but who were not necessarily familiar with or thinking about the Lake Flato brand during their online research. These un-branded keyword phrases can therefore be used as the centerpiece of a social media campaign to help drive additional search traffic from potential customers looking for architecture services. This is a key method that can expand the base of customers to your company.

Google offers a variety of free keyword tools to help you discover the best keyword phrases to optimize your website and social media campaign. Type in words related to your services and Google will pull up a list of related phrases. For best results, look for a few top phrases that offer a high search volume with low competition. WordTracker.com and MarketSamurai.com are also great keyword discovery tools and have a small monthly fee associated after your free trial expires.

Another way to really narrow in on best keyword phrases to use throughout your social media efforts is to set up a Google AdWords[3] account. This will allow you to not only see which keywords deliver the most quality traffic to your website but which keyword phrases actually convert to quality leads. Google charges a few dollars per click. The exact price per click can vary and depends on how competitive the keyword phrases are. Google does makes it easy to set a budget you feel comfortable with. We recommend starting with a test budget of a few hundred dollars to help you determine the best keyword phrases.

Measuring search engine optimization

Engagement is not only a cornerstone to building lasting relationships with your online connections but it will also help increase your search engine ranking and exposure online. In early 2011, Google's algorithms were updated to give companies with the most "social authority" more weight in the search engines. Social authority is not only measured by how many friends, followers or fans you have but also by how much engagement each of your posts receives. For example: a Facebook post that receives several comments and likes, a tweet that gets re-tweeted and a blog post that receives many link backs and comments are all ways Google measures how much authority you have on the social web. Combining these great

---

3   google.com/adwords

comments, tweets and posts with your core keyword phrases will help your website, blog and social profile show up in the research path of your next potential client looking for your services.

This increase in search ranking is one of the primary outcomes that HPD Architecture is hoping for through their social media campaigns.

"We are measuring the effectiveness of our social media campaign by increased unique visits to our website, increased personal referrals for prospective clients or projects leads and improvement of where our online listing(s) appear in the search engines (i.e., first page of Google) associated with specific keyword searches," explains Laura Davis, vice president and director of marketing for HPD.

Tracking through URL shorteners

URL shorteners provide an easy way to make those lengthy blog URLs and long company landing page website addresses appear cleaner. They are also essential for use in Twitter, where tweets must be kept to 140 characters or less. There are hundreds of URL shortener services available. We recommend you use one that will also help you track activity. After you sign up for an account, Bit.ly and Goo.gl both provide useful statistics on click activity. And better yet, these two sites are recognized by Google's search algorithm as trusted sources. This means that using them to shorten your URL will help your link building efforts as they relate to your search engine optimization strategy.

Facebook Insights

Facebook Insights is the analytics program that is associated with Facebook pages. While Google Analytics will show you that traffic came to your website as a result of Facebook, Insights will show you what posts actually generated the most engagement with your page. You can view the interactions each of your posts has and even review the time of day you made the post so you can determine the best time to post content based on your audiences usage habits.

WordPress and YouTube also have their own versions of in-page analytics so you can monitor how people react to your content. Twitter and LinkedIn announced that they will be releasing their versions of analytics in the future as well.

The most exciting thing about social media is that it happens in real time. This means you can test multiple types of messaging and gain instant feedback on what works and what doesn't. Try different hashtags and industry questions on Twitter. Post a hot topic or surprising industry fact on Facebook. Then use multiple analytic tools to monitor and track the interactions to determine engagement, interest and health and ultimately discover which activities lead to completing your business goals in the most time efficient and cost effective way. Using tracking tools will help you understand quickly what resonates with your audience and encourages them to share your information on other networks. With that said, it's important to note that just because one particular comment works to generate leads one week does not automatically mean it will generate the same results the next week. Social media involves real people and real interactions which means outcomes are not always predictable, even with the most sophisticated tools. However, the tools available will help you build healthier, more engaging networks in the long term and in the end, help you cut through the noise and attain a better return on investment for your social media campaign goals. Just like building relationships in real life, social media marketing is not an overnight process; it's a long term commitment.

Arthur Nielsen once said, "The price of light is less than the cost of darkness." Quite simply, taking time to invest in social media analytics and understanding what your target audience wants is invaluable to your firm's financial success. Strategic, thoughtful and ongoing listening and analysis of the social web is critical. Patience and timing are key. Understanding digital analytics and social media measurements and how that data impacts your business goals will provide you with the ability to make better decisions and become more accountable for your company's actions. At the end of the day, active social media monitoring will turn your firm into a better and more profitable company.

Chapter 8
The Future of Social Media

Step outside and you'll see that the digital world is already spilling out of our computer screens and quickly weaving itself into our daily, physical lives. According to Nielsen's May 2011 survey of mobile consumers in the U.S., 38 percent now own smartphones, allowing immediate access to the social web anytime, anywhere. And as smartphones continue to evolve into multi-functional devices they will take over tasks that used to require other objects. Some predict that these sleek handheld mobile devices will eventually replace such essentials as your wallet and keys and become a natural way of engaging with the physical world around us.

Architects, urban planners, engineers and building professionals should consider how such mobile technology will impact the design of buildings and space in the very near future. Just as we already see social media use of the jumbotron at concerts and baseball games engaging fans by encouraging public posts and photo uploads via their smartphones, we may see similar engagement in a less invasive way on libraries, park benches, museums, schools and public buildings. Imagine being able to learn about a building, city or landmark with a click of your phone and connecting to like-minded friends who share your interest in the subject. This technology is already in place and is expected to become even more mainstream according to Andrew Blum in the April 2011 Metropolis Magazine[1].

"Our experience of the world around us has changed to a degree not seen since the arrival of trains and cars", writes Blum. "The presence of 'the Net' —— by which I loosely mean all two-way, personal media — has become as much a factor in our experience of space as the play of light and shadow on a wall or the cultural accretions that dignify local architecture styles."

We are already seeing the mixing of networked media and built spaces. Local Projects, a New York-based firm that designs media for museums and public spaces, designed the arrangement of the names of the September 11 victims and the associated web and mobile interfaces for The National September 11th Memorial and Museum at the World Trade Center.

Technology was the only way to organize the names according to the groups they were affiliated with and honor the adjacencies requested

1   http://www.metropolismag.com/story/20110414/here-but-not-here

by the victims' next-of-kin and surviving colleagues. According to the memorial website[2], "Some requests were between relatives and friends; others were between people who had just met, but who responded together as events unfolded." This arrangement adds to the meaning of the memorial, but because it isn't an intuitive system, the memorial makes the final arrangement of names, as well as brief biographical information as provided by next-of-kin, available as an application for smartphones, tablet computers and electronic kiosks.

You have probably seen Quick Response (QR) codes on packaging and products in stores. QR codes are black and white boxes that look like bar codes and that function similar to radio frequency identification (RFID) tags. You see QR codes in more and more places — on the pages of print magazines or on outdoor billboards, for example. You can get a QR reader application on your smartphone, like the free ScanLife or any of the dozens of other free or paid versions, and then scan the QR code (or regular barcode) and gain additional information such as a coupon or even opt into a contest.

As the QR code's popularity grows, so does its size. To promote a new dinosaur exhibit, a person-sized QR code was displayed on one of the walls of Madison Square Garden in New York, N.Y. Passersby scanned the enormous code using a QR code reader application on their mobile phone for the opportunity to upload their "biggest dinosaur roar" in a contest. Anyone who entered a roar had a chance to win tickets to the popular Walking with Dinosaurs show at Madison Square Garden.

---

2   http://www.911memorial.org/

QR technology is now finding its way into the built environment. The City of New York's department of buildings is now including QR codes on all of its construction and electrical permits[3]. In a prepared statement, Mayor Bloomberg stated, "New Yorkers expect to be able to gather information instantly, and the use of QR codes will allow them to get all information about construction work while standing on the sidewalk." Users with smartphones will have access to all the information about the construction ranging from the site manager's phone number to the contractor's possible prior violations.

We are also seeing more subtle uses of QR codes in our physical world. Realtors are embedding QR codes on "For Sale" signs and buildings. By scanning the QR code, interested buyers can view floorplans, prices and even videos of a building immediately on their smartphones as they stand near the sign.

In the future, we could see QR codes as common features on signage for famous landmarks or city buildings. Visitors could easily scan the code to know more about the creation of the building, its uses and the names of the architects, engineers and other professionals involved. Think of it as a digital signature or business card for your company thus bringing the building industry to the fore-front, rather than behind the scenes.

As more people use smartphones to engage with the physical world in a networked way, they will begin to leave more and more digital breadcrumbs about where they have been, what they like and how they behave on a daily basis. City and state governments are already recognizing the power of these tools for interacting with constituents

3 http://www.customqrcodes.com/story/30/New-York-Introduces-QR-Codes-on-All-Building-Permits

—— and the power of the data that this creates. Urban planners, engineers and architects will gain more insight into how people move about cities and their surrounding regions to be able to offer more targeted designs to accommodate a modern lifestyle. They will also have even more data to back up their creative ideas on use of space and design.

Growth of location-based social networking

"The piece that is missing from the AEC social media realm is the incorporation of 'places' and 'checking in' such as on Foursquare and Facebook places," says HMC's Nick Bryan. "We are still trying to understand how it can be incorporated into our social media strategy and recognize that it is the next wave of social interaction."

"The A/E industry will eventually need to jump on board and develop ways to interact with this strand of social media," continued Janice Endsley, HMC public relations coordinator. "To us, it seems as if this approach would be a good fit for the industry, as the industry is designing and building the places that people eventually 'check in' to."

In case you are not familiar with location-based social networks like Foursquare, it is a web site that allows you to "check in" via your GPS-enabled mobile devices such as your smartphone or iPad. Once you check in, you can see if any of your friends or coworkers have checked in to nearby venues. You can also gain rewards for checking in at specific locations. For example, if the location owner has "claimed the venue" and is using Foursquare as a marketing channel, you may get a special message or unlock a secret coupon. Foursquare also doubles as a social game. People try to check in to as many places as possible to earn badges and become the virtual "mayor" of a specific place. In some cases, becoming a mayor or having certain badges will earn them discounts and coupons, in other cases, it is simply a contest in order to online recognition for having the most check ins at a particular place. This idea of check ins is gaining momentum. According to the Foursquare blog, the site grew 3,400% from 2009–2010, with the 6 millionth user signing up in January 2011.

The AIA is already using FourSquare as a way to showcase architects' works to the general public and give them exposure.

"How often will 'non-architect Jane Smith' check in to a venue and discover the architect of the site or even know that the venue won a design award?" asks Sybil Walker Barnes, director of social media for The AIA. Barnes goes on to explain how architects can get involved to support AIA National on Foursquare, "It's a simple formula: they continue creating great architecture and we'll continue to showcase it on Foursquare." Barnes was quick to point out that location-based engagement is in its infancy, "but I think it could be a possibility for a solo practitioner or firm to use to connect with their followers. The explosion of people using their mobile devices to actively engage with locations in entirely new ways opens new doors and new ways of thinking about how to reach our audiences."

Another location-based technology that is creating new ways for designers and planners to speak directly to the public when they are in the actual designed space is New York, New York-based Broadcastr[4]. This social media platform lets users record, index, listen to and share audio content online through their mobile device, tablet or personal computers. Users are fed content relevant to where they are that moment.

We spoke with Andy Hunter, Broadcastr CEO and co-founder about this platform and how it can be applied to the built environment. "Story and place have always been intimately connected. Designers know this better than probably anyone else. By using audio, Broadcastr lets you access information about the world without pulling you out of it — your hands and eyes are free."

For example, the Bryant Park Corporation has contributed stories about Manhattan's Town Square on Broadcastr, so as a user walks through Bryant Park they can get background on the park's famous chairs or hear about the Thursday night yoga program or the story regarding how the park hosted an educational vegetable garden to help New Yorkers grow their own food during World War I.

---

4   http://beta.broadcastr.com

Hunter offered an idea to designers, "Because anyone can upload a story to Broadcastr, the designer can invite the people in his/her space to contribute their own stories. The archive becomes a living thing, growing with each mark left by an individual." Users that download the Broadcastr app for their mobile device can not only listen to content based on where they stand but they can also record their story and contribute it to the platform without leaving the space.

The reputation economy is coming

"The reputation economy is an environment where brands are built based on how they are perceived online and the promise they deliver offline," Dan Schawbel wrote in his February 2011 "Personal Branding" blog[5] for Forbes. Schawbel predicts that your online reputation will surpass your paper resume. "I believe that in order to compete in the global economy, you have to have an online personal brand. After you create that presence, you have to maintain it throughout the course of your entire life, before someone else does it for you."

Most employers already understand the impact of an online reputation. According to a January 2011 Microsoft Survey[6], 80% of hiring managers use online reputation information in their hiring process and 70% said they rejected candidates due to information they discovered about them online.

---

5 http://blogs.forbes.com/danschawbel/2011/02/21/5-reasons-why-your-online-presence-will-replace-your-resume-in-10-years/
6 http://www.microsoft.com/privacy/dpd/default.aspx

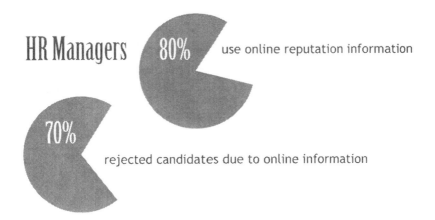

HR Managers **80%** use online reputation information

70% rejected candidates due to online information

More companies are realizing the value employees with a great online reputation can bring to a business. Salesforce's CEO Mark Benioff told Forbes Editor Victoria Barret in an on-stage interview at a GigaOM's Net:Work conference about his idea of using technologies to gauge an employee's online reputation and influence to increase an employee's pay. During the interview, he suggested that employees who make an impact with online contributions should be rewarded with extra bonuses.

A new online social game called Empire Avenue[7] allows you to take stock in the future value of online influencers. The social network functions like a stock exchange where you can buy and sell shares of other members' profiles using virtual currency called "eaves." The value of a person's profile increases the more they participate in social networks. Although currently only an online game for fake money, you can see where this trend is heading. Online influence is valuable. And predicting the future online influence of employees and coworkers is even more valuable.

---

7   empireavenue.com

Until real money is at stake, this is an interesting way to get an understanding of the influence and value of some members of specific industries and what trends lead to buying and selling stock in thought leaders.

The critical role of influencers in your social media strategy

As more and more people engage in social media, we predict they will rely more heavily on the recommendations of primary influencers or thought leaders to help them sort through the millions of messages and separate the noise from information that is relevant to their particular lives.

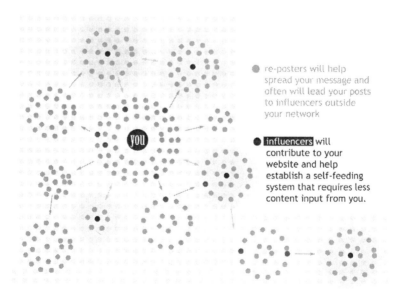

re-posters will help spread your message and often will lead your posts to influencers outside your network

influencers will contribute to your website and help establish a self-feeding system that requires less content input from you.

a healthy community

Technology companies are already seeing the need for firms to find and gain access to such influential social media users. Currently each company offers different algorithms to predict and identify "influence" over a particular group. These tools provide insight beyond how many followers or friends a person may have but calculate influence by how many people retweet or comment on that person's post. Some websites worth watching include Klout[8] and MPact[9]. Klout, which received $8.5 million in new funding in early 2011, is an application that measures a person's online influence by reach, amplification probability and network influence. MPact is a similar application but allows you to find influencers by specific keywords or industry.

Big brands are already jumping on this data. Disney used Klout to identify 500 influential online moms. Once identified, Disney sent the moms passes to a free screening of the new movie Tangled and mailed their children a kit of Tangled merchandise. Leapster, an educational learning system designed by Emeryville, California-based LeapFrog Enterprises[10], identified top influential parents in the social space and now pays them to write regular blogs. Luxury hotels in Vegas are using similar data to offer special incentives and preferential treatment to customers with the biggest social influence.

As you build your marketing plans for the architecture and building industry, consider using these tools to discover who your most influential customers are and how you can encourage them to talk about your brand in a positive way with their followers.

---

8   www.klout.com
9   www.mpact.com
10   www.leapfrog.com

How social media will impact journalism

With the explosion of blogs, we have already seen how the everyday person can impact journalism and even compete with recognized, long-standing traditional news media. However, as more and more companies get on board with social media in a strategic way, we expect to see more "citizen journalism" and "brand journalism," where thoughts and ideas are shaped by industry leaders and online advocates. Social media marketers already have a name for fans who spread a company's values and thoughts: brand evangelists.

Further customization of social networks and tools

As more and more companies use Facebook, we predict we will see a growing need for additional widgets and customization tools to make Facebook pages do more. From free Facebook apps to paid monthly services like North Social[11], we will see more and more companies begin to customize their Facebook pages to engage in more powerful ways with customers and fans.

In 2011, Facebook announced the average media site that integrated a Facebook like button or other Facebook plugin saw a 300% increase in referral traffic[12]. And the type of online audience that uses social networks like Facebook, continue to be the most engaged. Facebook reported that visitors who sign in with Facebook on The Huffington Post view 22% more pages and spend eight minutes longer there than the average reader. Those who sign in to NHL.com with

---

11   www.northsocial.com
12   http://searchengineland.com/by-the-numbers-how-facebook-says-likes-social-plugins-help-websites-76061

Facebook spend 85% more time and read 90% more articles than the average user. The stats go on and on from major companies to small businesses: they are finding that the social network-engaged internet user most often becomes their most loyal and valuable customer. As more and more companies and major media sites entrench social plugins into the technology we use, the use and reach of such social media channels will continue to expand.

an integrated like button = 300% increase in referral traffic

More connected buildings and spaces in the future

Great architecture should reflect the people and environment around it. As people are more and more entrenched in technology to perform their daily functions, architects, urban designers and city planners will have to further incorporate technology into designs to not only stay relevant but to develop useful structures and landscapes for today's public.

We are already seeing the Internet enter home technologies outside of the computer screen. Depending on your cable television provider, you may already have the capability of recording your favorite television show on your home digital video recorder while away from home via your office computer or your smartphone. In fact, some cable television providers even allow you to access Facebook and YouTube through your digital television so you can chat with friends or leave comments on a television show's social page or forum while you watch your favorite programs.

And for people who want to have more control of their home while they are away, they can opt for installing smart home technology which allows them to virtually interact with anything that is electronic in the home beyond just the television. Imagine having your favorite song playing when you walk in the door or the lights in your house automatically dimming when you turn on a movie. The costs associated with installing such systems start at around $10,000 while Bill Gates' customized version was estimated to cost $100 million. The possibilities of connecting the physical world to the virtual are just beginning.

Social media technology is all around us and will continue to be more and more woven into our everyday routines even when we are away from the computer. In 2011, New York City Mayor Michael Bloomberg announced that the city now provides free Wi-Fi in all its parks[13]. As digital content becomes more easily accessed in public spaces —— whether through a Wi-Fi connected laptop, tablet or your mobile phone —— "Designers should take social media into account as they think through ways that people use space," recommends Broadcastr's Andy Hunter. "Part of the beauty of the technology is

13   http://www.nyc.gov/portal/site/nycgov/menuitem.
c0935b9a57bb4ef3daf2f1c701c789a0/index.jsp?pageID=mayor_press_
release&catID=1194&doc_name=http%3A%2F%2Fwww.nyc.gov%2Fhtml%2Fom%2Fht
ml%2F2011a%2Fpr202-11.html&cc=unused1978&rc=1194&ndi=1)

that it's digital; it can be layered onto any project without physical changes."

It is an exciting time to be an architect, designer, engineer and planner as the possibilities for helping to create innovative spaces that engage both the virtual and physical world will put you at the forefront of the next chapter in human interaction with the natural and built environments. Before you can design and build for the networked world, you must truly experience and engage in it yourself. Get started with the freeware and cheapware social media tools readily available today and use them to share ideas, learn, and market yourself, your company and its thought leaders. Technology is evolving quickly to meet the way that we live, work and play. If we don't apply ourselves in learning and using the tools we have today, we won't be open to social, political and organizational innovations that occur tomorrow.

Glossary

Analytics
Website analytics is the collection, presentation and analysis of information about site users' behavior for the purposes of reporting, learning from and optimizing a website for an improved user experience.

App
App is smart phone slang (initiated by the iPhone) for an application that performs a specific function on your personal device or computer.

Blog
The term "blog" comes from "web log". A blog is an online journal that is interactive and allows visitors to leave comments. Blogs often provide commentary or news on a particular subject, although some function as personal online diaries. Bloggers can add new text, images and videos to their blogs without having to know any web programming, which is the primary reason for the rapid growth in popularity of blogging among all types of Internet users.

Blogger
A blogger is the title given to the person writing blog entries.

Blogging
Blogging is a term used to describe the act of writing a blog.

Click-Throughs
A click-through is a type of digital metric that refers to the act of literally clicking on a link and going to a web page. When talking about click-throughs in online advertising, The click-through rate

(CTR) is a metric for measuring success. The CTR for an online ad is defined as the number of clicks on an advertisement divided by the number of times the ad is shown.

Crowdsourcing

Crowdsourcing refers to an open call for input or contributions on specified subject, product or solution to perform business-related tasks that would otherwise have been done by the company itself. Social media simplifies crowdsourcing by providing access to a larger pool of potential respondents.

Digital Metrics

Digital metrics refers to marketing activity and actions you can measure online, such as traffic to your web site, click-throughs from a banner ad or opens from an email message. Digital metrics can be tracked through a variety of web analytics programs.

Direct Message

In Twitter you can send a private 140 character message, called a direct message, to anyone who follows you, but you can only receive messages from people whom you also follow.

Embedding

Embedding is the act of inserting a line of code into web content for the purpose of sharing a video, photo or image that is hosted somewhere else.

Facebook Friends

Facebook friend is a term that describes the people in your personal Facebook network. Facebook friends are those people you have approved and granted access to view your Facebook updates. Facebook friends are able to view and comment on each other's Facebook pages.

Facebook Plugin

A Facebook plugin is an embeddable social feature that can be integrated in your website with a line of HTML. Because the social plugin is hosted by Facebook, it is personalized for all users who are currently logged into Facebook, even if they are visiting your site for the first time.

Feed

See RSS Feed

Guest Blogging

Guest blogging is the act of contributing one or more blog posts to blog owned and managed by a third party.

Hashtags

Twitter hashtags were developed as a way to create topic groups on Twitter. Using hashtags provides an easy way to locate and keep track of conversations on specific topics of interest. Twitter hashtags begin with # and are followed by a keyword phrase such as #design or #build.

Keywords

Keywords is a term used when someone enters specific words or phrases into a search field on a website describing more information they hope to find. Keywords are also used by search engines in order to find, categorize and rank web pages so they can display the best option for internet users looking for related information.

Keyword–friendly

Keyword-friendly is a term used by search engine optimization professionals when describing a web page, post or comment online that was written for the search engines. In other words, specific keyword phrases were added to the page or post in hopes that the search engines will find and rank it.

Klout Score

A Klout score is one way to measure a person's online influence. The score ranges from 1 -100 and is based on calculating variables from different social channels including Faceook and Twitter. Developed by a San Francisco, California-based company called Klout, the Klout score measures the size of a person's online audience, likelihood that a person's message will get amplified or shared online, and overall influence of that person's engaged audience.

Like

Like is a term used by Facebook to show support of a website, product, photo, comment or other type of online information. For a user to like something online, they must be either on Facebook or viewing a website that uses the Facebook like plugin while logged into their Facebook account. The online content the user liked will then show up in their Facebook profile.

Lists

In Twitter you can organize the accounts you follow by categorizing them in lists. Lists can be made public or kept private. Others can subscribe to or follow your public lists that interest them.

Modified Tweet

Similar to a retweet (RT). Indicate your tweet is a modified tweet (MT) when you are significantly altering the original tweet, by using MT instead of RT. (see Retweet.)

Pay-Per-Click Campaign

A pay-per-click campaign is a type of online ad buy where the advertiser only pays when a web user clicks on their advertisement. The most common pay-per-click campaigns are offered by search engines such as MSN, Yahoo! or Google AdWords. In a search engine pay-per-click campaign, an advertiser can bid on keywords that they want their ad and website link to be found under. Advertisers can bid anywhere from $0.05 to upwards of $10+ per click. They are only charged when a user clicks on the ad and visits their web site.

Posting

Posting refers to the act of adding content including a comment, photo or other information to a website or social network.

Retweet

Retweet is a term used to describe the act of re-posting some else's tweet to your own Twitter feed. Having your tweet retweeted is desirable because it helps your tweet gain exposure on other people's Twitter accounts and reach more people online. The format is "RT @username" where username is the twitter handle of the person you are retweeting.

RSS Feeds

RSS feeds (or really simple syndication) is a type of web feed format used to easily and automatically publish frequently updated information such as news headlines and blog updates. RSS feeds are read by using software called an RSS reader or aggregator, which can be website or desktop based or work on various mobile devices.

Search Engines

A search engine is an online tool that allows a user to search for information on the World Wide Web through a variety of keyword phrases. Google and Bing are two examples of search engines.

Search Engine Optimization

Search engine optimization is the process of organizing a website and its content to improve the chance that it will be included near the top of search engine rankings by considering search engines' criteria for gathering, evaluating and ranking information.

Share

A share in social media refers to any way a user chooses to pass content along to their online social networks. Many blogs and websites have social plugins that make sharing easy by providing immediate access to the user's Twitter, Facebook or other social media profiles for the purpose of sharing the link.

Smart Phone

A smart phone is a hand-held device that offers more functionality beyond standard mobile phone services. Common features include email, web access, and the ability to add apps that perform a specific function.

Social Bookmarking

Social bookmarking is a way for internet users to note, organize and store favorite websites, pages and online resources on a platform that can be located anywhere.

Spam

Spam refers to unsolicited bulk email, junk mail or posts,. Commercial email that a recipient has not requested or "opted in" for is considered spam.

Tag

A tag is a keyword added to a blog post, image, photo or video for the purposes of helping visitors find content that is related to their interests.

Tag Cloud

A tag cloud is a visual representation of the most commonly used or most popular tags on a particular site.

Thought Leader

A thought leader refers to someone who has influential and innovative ideas related to a specific industry that merit attention and discussion.

Troll

A troll refers to a person who is overly critical and posts hurtful, damaging and/or negative comments anonymously on the social web.

Tweets

A tweet is the term used for a post that is made on Twitter.

Tweet Chat

A tweet chat is a pre arranged, topic-focused gathering on Twitter. Tweet chat's often have a leader or moderator and sometimes a predetermined agenda. Participants contribute to and follow the discussion through tweets that include a pre-established hashtag (like #AECSM, which takes place Tuesdays at 1pm PST).

Tweetup

A tweetup is an organized or impromptu in-person gathering of people who interact on Twitter.

Twitter Followers

A Twitter follower is someone who has opted to receive the tweets posted by another Twitter user.

Webcasting

The action of using the web to deliver live or previously recorded broadcasts.

Webinar

A webinar is an online seminar with presentation materials available through an online interface. Typically, attendees register in advance, log in at the specified time for access to live audio and presentation materials. Most webinars include a Q&A feature that allows participants to pose questions during or at the end of the presentations.

Widgets

A web widget is a small application that can be installed on a web page, often with a few lines of code. They are typically created in DHTML, JavaScript or Adobe Flash. Online tools such as date/time clocks, stock market tickers and daily weather are all examples of widgets.

Wi-Fi

Wi-Fi refers to a wireless internet connection or wireless networking standards

CPSIA information can be obtained at www.ICGtesting.com
Printed in the USA
LVOW080342190312

273654LV00005B/1/P